We all know how it started: A teenage girl from Pennsylvania moved to Nashville and rose to the top of the country music charts. In 2006, Taylor Swift's story began—and with it, so did ours as Swifties.

The Story of Us is a heartfelt journey through Swiftie history, capturing the evolution of a fandom that has stood the test of time. Told through the lens of personal experiences, this book chronicles the rise of a fandom that has remained fiercely loyal through every era. From calling radio stations to request "Tim McGraw," to those unforgettable moments on Tumblr when Taylor and fans felt like friends, to surviving the Ticketmaster war—we've been there. We've learned life lessons, traded friendship bracelets, mastered time zone math to tune in to livestreams, and created a language only another Swiftie—or Taylor herself—could understand. But beyond all of these shared moments, what truly binds us is how Taylor's lyrics feel like they were written just for us—like reflections of our own stories.

This passionate and unique fandom has won awards and been intensely studied, but for the first time, fans can reminisce and celebrate what it means to be part of this life-changing community. A love letter written by a Swiftie for Swifties, *The Story of Us* ensures that our story will never be forgotten.

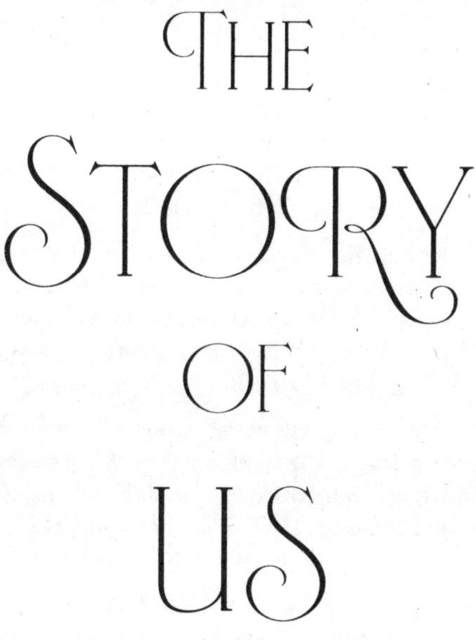

The Story of Us

How the Taylor Swift Fandom Changed Our Lives

Olivia Levin

Illustrations by Cian Halliwell

Simon & Schuster

NEW YORK AMSTERDAM/ANTWERP LONDON TORONTO

SYDNEY/MELBOURNE NEW DELHI

Simon & Schuster
1230 Avenue of the Americas
New York, NY 10020

First Simon & Schuster hardcover edition April 2026

SIMON & SCHUSTER and colophon are registered trademarks of Simon & Schuster, LLC

Interior design by Joy O'Meara
Decorative elements: © oblachko, © Kutukupretkw2, © Mcarrel/Dreamstime.com

Manufactured in the United States of America

3 5 7 9 10 8 6 4 2

Library of Congress Cataloging-in-Publication Data has been applied for.

ISBN 978-1-6680-9292-7
ISBN 978-1-6680-9294-1 (ebook)

For Mom and Dad,
who took me to my first Taylor concert,
traveled with me to shows, and never stopped
encouraging me to chase my wildest dreams

Taylor,

Thank you for chasing your dream of becoming a songwriter and performer. That decision changed so many lives, including mine. In following your path, you helped me find one of my own, one I never would've discovered otherwise. Wherever my life or career takes me, I'll never forget that it all started with you and your music. More than anything, thank you for creating what I truly believe is the most joy-filled, loving community in the world. What began as a simple fan account has become a lifeline. This community gave me purpose, opportunity, adventure, and healing, and I don't know where I'd be without it. I know I'm just one of millions who feel the same. That's the power of what you've built. It stretches far beyond your music. Thank you for caring so deeply and for sharing your heart, your courage, and your spark. Should this book make its way into your hands, may it remind you of the magic you've created. I hope that no matter how much time passes, we all keep holding on to the memories, just like they'll always hold on to us.

WATCH HILL
1989

CHAPTER ONE

It's Me, Hi!

As we grow older, our interests and personalities evolve. We all go through phases, or eras even, as we search for who we are in this life. But ever since I was thirteen years old, I've known I would be a Swiftie for eternity. Many passions have come and gone, but none of them have captured my heart the way this fandom has. We gave Taylor our love and loyalty, and in return, she has given us the soundtrack to our lives, a role model who's paved the way, and above all, a community. Being part of this fandom has shown me time and time again how a shared love for one artist can unite people from every corner of the globe. We have turned fandom into something timeless and transcendent, a living legacy of connection and stories that will be passed down for generations to come.

This book is my love letter to you, the ones who gave me purpose, friendship, and a kind of joy I didn't even know was possible. You've shown me the beauty of connection, the purpose within passion, and the love that can be found in the most unexpected places. If you've been here from the beginning, get ready to take a walk down memory lane: to the albums, the eras, the late-night livestreams, the theories, the chaos, the tears, the laughter, the inside jokes, the happiness, the fun, and the magic. You were there for all of it, and I hope these pages take you back to those moments. And if you're new here, welcome. I hope this book helps you feel like you were part of it all along, because in a way, you were. We all carry a piece of this story that is still being written.

My story with Taylor starts at eight years old, when I first heard "Love Story" on the radio. I loved the storytelling, the romance, and the feelings it stirred in me, even if I didn't yet know who Romeo and Juliet were. At thirteen, my relationship with Taylor's music deepened. Her music was no longer just something I listened to casually. Instead, it became something I felt in my bones. Maybe that shift came with growing older, as I started to understand her lyrics on a more personal level and saw my own emotions reflected in her songs. I vividly remember sitting on Charlestown Beach in Rhode Island one night in August 2014, watching the "Shake It Off" music video on my friend's phone for the first time. This was the moment I realized that from then on, I was no longer going to be a casual fan. I was going *full throttle.* It was a poetic place for my *epiphany*, considering just over three years later, I'd be hanging out with Taylor on another, more well-known Rhode Island beach in Watch Hill.

I dove headfirst into catching up on years of YouTube videos and fandom lore I had missed. I watched her early vlogs and every interview she had done, and I began immersing myself in the online fan community. To this day, my childhood best friend reminds me of how lucky I am that she put up with me during this transitional period. You see, when we would have sleepovers, I would pretty much force her to read lyrics and watch music videos with me, thinking she'd appreciate them as much as I did. I eventually became socially aware enough to understand that not everyone wanted to sit around and talk about Taylor all night. At the time, I was just ecstatic to have found an artist whose music resonated with me—even if I hadn't lived much of what she was singing about yet. I hadn't experienced heartbreak or epic love stories, but somehow, I still felt the weight of every word.

What first drew me to Taylor was how unapologetically authentic she was. She never dimmed her light or tried to mold herself into anyone else's idea of what a star should be. Whether people thought she was too emotional, too dramatic, or not "cool" enough, she never compromised her identity to fit a more traditionally marketable image. She was uninterested in doing the same thing everyone else was doing. I admired her just as much as I was inspired by her. And while it was Taylor who reeled me into being a Swiftie, what made me stay was the realization that there were millions of people all around the world who felt the exact same way I did. They, too, connected to her and her lyrics in a way that made them feel seen, and suddenly, we had this incredible ability to find each other online. Even though social media has its downfalls, I've always believed that it was one of the greatest blessings for our community. It allowed us to connect, communicate, and form friendships with people across oceans. More than that, it played a huge role in building the bond we share with Taylor today.

In 2014, everyone was joining Instagram and Twitter, but it was also the era of Tumblr, which was typically used by bloggers, creatives, and niche-obsessed people. Taylor herself joined Tumblr in September 2014, so naturally, I did too. I chose the account name @swiftiesforeternity because, even though some people in my life assumed my newfound "hobby" was just a phase, I knew it wasn't. Taylor turned Tumblr into our community's safe space, away from the media and anyone else who loved to *rain on our parade*. Of course, I chatted with other fans about their favorite songs, but oftentimes we'd find ourselves talking about non-Taylor-related things too. I remember posting a photo of myself and saying that I was on my way to a tennis lesson. Taylor liked that post. In fact, she liked a lot of our posts that were unrelated to her, and I always thought it was her way of trying to relate to us on more than an artist-to-fan level. Whenever I told people that Taylor Swift was liking or re-blogging my posts, they would brush it off as it being her team and not actually her. It was always hard to explain how we just knew it was her. Something about the way she wrote those endearingly nerdy, millennialesque hashtags under every caption gave her away instantly. As a fan who was familiar with her early 2000s MySpace blogging days, I recognized that it couldn't have been anyone but her. Over the years, Taylor interacted with me from time to time—liking my posts and, one day, following me on Tumblr. It really was the golden age of Tumblr for Swifties.

It was a stark contrast to what came next—2016 was, without a doubt, the most intense year to be a Swiftie. It felt like everyone had turned against her. Suddenly, being a fan wasn't cool anymore, and Taylor disappeared from the public eye, leaving us all uneasy and anxious, wondering if, or when, she'd return to music. The silence was deafening. More than anything, we just wanted her to be okay. The headlines were brutal, and the media frenzy felt toxic. Still, we kept our fan accounts active, posting and sharing memories to keep the Swiftie spirit alive until she returned. Through it all our community held tight, and long story short: *We survived.*

In 2017, the drought was over, and she came back *stronger than a nineties trend*. She wasn't going to let the public opinion take away what she had worked so hard to build. Instead, she reclaimed her place by releasing an album that felt like it was meant only for us to understand. The era felt personal, almost sacred. The shows were packed with die-hard, chronically online Swifties, and Taylor seemed to recognize more of us on Tumblr and in person than ever before, not only by our faces but by our usernames too.

I Was Enchanted to Meet You

On October 7, 2017, Taylor voted yes on my Instagram poll where I asked my followers if they thought the *reputation* era would live up to previous ones. She then responded with a smiley-face emoji to a selfie I posted on my story. All in one day. Although I was over the moon about her knowing who I was, I really didn't think much more of it. I just assumed she was excitedly interacting with us following her break. Five days later, on October 12, 2017, I was at my senior high school internship when I received a message on Tumblr from her team, Taylor Nation, who asked where

I lived, my contact information, and how old I was. I immediately responded but didn't get a message back from them. That is, until the next day at school, when I got a call from an unknown number. I picked up, and the woman on the other end said, "Hi, is this Olivia?" I knew right away what it was for and could barely contain my excitement. Rumors had already begun swirling in the fandom regarding a Secret Session. I quickly replied, "Yes!" She continued, "Taylor saw how big of a fan you are and would like to invite you to a private event in Rhode Island next Thursday. Are you interested?" Was I interested? Was she kidding? Known for oversharing, I immediately launched into how I could definitely get the day off school, and how my mom, who was also a Swiftie, would come with me. She laughed and said, "That's great! We'll send you an email with the details by Sunday." But Sunday came and went with no email. By Monday night, I was panicking. Could I still go without the official details? I assumed the event would be at Taylor's house since the woman from her team mentioned Rhode Island. Should I just show up in Rhode Island and hope for the best? *No, Olivia. That would be weird.* Thankfully, my dad told me to check my spam email. And there it was. An email with all the information I needed, including a code word, "A-Team," to say upon arrival. I didn't know at the time that it was hinting at "End Game," a new collaboration with Ed Sheeran.

On October 19, I woke up knowing I was going to meet my idol, the girl whose music had carried me through some of the most emotional times of my life. It was surreal. As a seventeen-year-old, I wasn't sure how I would act or what I would say to her. I didn't want to be generic and say the same thing she hears a hundred times a day, but also, what do you say to someone you already know so much about? Clearly, I'm a perpetual overthinker—I probably should've just bonded with her over that.

I had my hair and makeup professionally done before getting in the car and heading to Watch Hill. Even though it's a popular beach town, it was late October, so the streets were almost eerily deserted. We pulled into a random parking lot where a few vans, a folding table, and a small group of people were waiting. After my mom and I checked in using the code word, they collected our phones and sealed them in ziplock bags. No phones, no wallets, nothing. Honestly, Taylor Swift is the only person I'd abandon all basic safety measures for without hesitation. My mom and I climbed into one of the vans with a few other Swifties, and the van immediately turned into a dance party. We were singing and dancing around so intensely that the whole vehicle was bouncing up and down. You know those moments that instantly become core memories, the kind you feel yourself holding on to as they happen? Well, I had one of those when my mom looked over at me in the van and said, "Take this all in, it's rare and special."

As we approached the gate, there it was: Holiday House. The closer we got, the more you could feel the energy shift. We all knew something life-changing was about to unfold. We entered through the garage, where we were scanned by metal detectors. And suddenly what I had been daydreaming about since that call was here. It was time. I made my way up the stairs and into the kitchen, casually wandering around while admiring the family photos on the walls. Sure, we all have family pictures in our homes, but something about seeing those made me realize just how normal she was. In one of the rooms, there was food waiting for us. I was far too nervous and full of anticipation to eat, though. I think I took a bite of one chicken nugget just so I could say I ate in Taylor Swift's house.

Eventually, I made my way out to the deck overlooking East Beach—one of the beaches I grew up visiting with friends and family. Many New Englanders vacation there, and a fun fact the locals always share is that if you look up from the shore, you can see Taylor's house perched above. The beach was completely empty that day, but I couldn't help imagining myself sitting there, like I had done so many times as a child, gazing up at where I was now standing. Never in a million years did I think I'd be looking down at it instead. Scott Swift, also known as Papa Swift, came out onto the deck and started sharing stories about Taylor—some funny, some heartfelt, and all completely unknown to the public, like the times she discreetly visited fans in hospitals just to brighten their day. We lingered on the deck, soaking in every word, before slowly making our way into the kitchen, still buzzing from the stories we'd just heard. Then Taylor's younger brother, Austin Swift, appeared, and all I remember is him adorably babbling about his love for *Game of Thrones*. Taylor was still upstairs getting ready, but I knew we were getting closer to seeing her when Andrea Swift, whom most fans lovingly call Mama Swift, walked into the kitchen. The other Swifties and I chatted with her, sharing how much her daughter's music had touched our lives. I'm sure that, as a parent, you could never hear that too much.

The doors to the main living room swung open, and we all filed in with a mixture of nerves and awe. My mom and I settled onto floor cushions placed in the front and just slightly to the right of a large armchair, the unmistakable focal point where it was clear Taylor would be sitting. As the room filled with chatter and excitement, someone started singing "Fearless," and within seconds the entire group joined in. Scott and Andrea sat behind us with smiles on their faces, waiting for their daughter to appear and make dreams come true simply with her presence. We weren't even halfway through the song when Taylor came sprinting down the stairs, bursting into the room with a glowing smile and a bubbly "Hey guys!" The room erupted in cheers. No words have ever felt big enough to convey the feeling I had in this moment, but we were all in utter disbelief. She began by introducing herself, as always. "I'm Taylor," she said, grabbing a glass of white wine and catching us up on where she'd been over the past year. It felt like story time. She had written an album that, on the surface, seemed like a drastic shift into darkness compared to her past eras, but really, it captured the fragile beauty of falling in love when everything else felt uncertain. She kicked things off by showing us a rough cut of the ". . . Ready For It?" music video, which hadn't been finalized yet. Then she did exactly what we had all been hoping for: She pressed play on her phone, showing us the entire *reputation* album in order and pausing before each track to explain the events, emotions, and sometimes the people that inspired them.

What struck me the most, apart from the brilliance of the album, was how much she had grown while she was away from the spotlight. She ultimately realized she could still have the big career she'd always dreamed of while also protecting her private life. Success and invasion of privacy were no longer a package deal. In the middle of the listening session, when "Look What You Made Me

Do" came on, Taylor suddenly called out a fan named Julia and asked her to stand up and sing the bridge with her. Since it was the lead single from the album, we all already knew every word. But Taylor had recently reposted a video of Julia screaming the bridge of the song on Tumblr, which made the moment even more special. Julia looked just as stunned as the rest of us, unable to believe that Taylor remembered her name. The two of them danced while the rest of us shouted "*'Cause she's dead!*" in perfect unison.

Once she had finished playing the album, we followed Andrea into another room. As I walked in and saw a piano, I had another one of those I'm-living-in-a-simulation moments. As Taylor walked into the room and we made eye contact, we smiled at each other. Her aura was magnetic—warm, radiant, with the type of presence that filled the room before a word was even spoken. She

came right up to me, hugged me, and thanked me for being there, then settled in front of the keyboard and asked if we wanted to hear her play a song. Of course, the answer was yes. I stood next to her as she graced our ears with "All Too Well." No, not the ten-minute version (it hadn't been released yet), but still nothing short of breathtaking. At one point, we joined in, singing softly alongside her. It wasn't loud or rehearsed, just intimate and magical. I still get chills thinking about it. Following her performance, she went back into the living room while the rest of us hung out in the piano room, chatting with Andrea. Meanwhile, Scott—to no one's surprise—was handing out guitar picks. One by one, we were called to meet Taylor in the living room.

There's something incredibly peculiar about meeting someone you've looked up to for years. Even though I knew she was just another normal human being—someone who gets tired, has bad days, and overthinks everything just like the rest of us—it was hard to fully grasp that in real time. For so long, she had existed in a completely different realm: music videos, award shows, online, and through lyrics that understood me better than I could sometimes understand myself. She wasn't just a "celebrity," she had been a big part of my life, even if she didn't know me. So when I was suddenly standing in front of her, breathing the same air, it felt like my brain was short-circuiting as I was attempting to reconcile the myth with the mortal. This was a one-of-a-kind experience for a seventeen-year-old small-town Connecticut girl, and it was an emotional whiplash in the very best way possible. But Taylor had a natural ease when it came to starstruck fans. She knew exactly how to make you feel comfortable and like you were just two old friends catching up.

As my mom and I approached her, all I heard was "Hey, sweetie!" Taylor hugged us and complimented our sense of style. We were both wearing black dresses to thematically represent the *reputation* album. Our conversation consisted of lots of back-and-forth banter. I asked her what perfume she was wearing because it smelled so amazing, and she said that it was Tom Ford's Tobacco Vanille but that her house's scent was Tom Ford's Santal Blush. To this day, whenever I catch either scent out in the wild, I'm instantly transported back. She thanked me for going all out and dressing up when I attended her *1989* Nashville shows with my mom and told me she had found me on both Tumblr and Instagram. As we were talking, she kept on hugging me out of the blue, and I distinctly remember her saying, "You're like a cute little button—I just want to hug you!" Then she turned to my mom and said, "Don't you just want to hug her all the time?" I was officially winning at life, and there was no way I wasn't making it everyone's problem at school the next day.

She radiated such a sweet and nurturing energy. After I spent that evening with her family, it became clear to me just how instrumental they were in keeping her grounded and as unaffected by fame as possible. She was still a kind and genuine soul, and there wasn't even a hint of conceit about her. When you talked to her, she made you feel like you were the only person in the room. She was fully present and gave you her undivided attention in a way that never felt forced or inauthentic. It always seemed like she truly wanted to hear what you had to say and make the moment about you, not her. My mom told her how inspiring it was that, despite all the media's negativity, she had still managed to find happiness and guard her private life from public scrutiny. And, as moms do, she told her to keep doing exactly that because they didn't deserve her. Taylor smiled and agreed, and we could both tell how much the support meant to her.

After about five more minutes of talking like we'd known each other forever, we were deciding on photo poses. I think she could tell I was nervous, so she asked me if I wanted to go sit in the beach chairs that her dad had brought out as props. She said, half joking, that he was a little sad no one was using them. Obviously, I said yes. She grabbed a couple of her Grammys off the shelf behind us and nonchalantly handed me the Album of the Year one for *1989*. "Damn, these are heavy!" I said. "They're heavier than you'd think, right?" she replied. We sat down and put our arms around each other. "Do you want to do a pouty face?" she asked. Before leaving, she hugged me one last time and said, "I'll see you online!" Nothing has been the same since.

It's worth noting that her cats Olivia and Meredith—named after characters from *Law & Order: SVU* and *Grey's Anatomy*, respectively—were part of that evening (the beautiful, blue-eyed Benjamin Button hadn't been born yet). I remember someone asking where they were, and Taylor responded that they were upstairs in her room, just in case any of us had allergies. She eventually brought Olivia downstairs for some photos. Later, already knowing about a girl named Emily and her health challenges through Tumblr, Taylor personally brought her upstairs to meet both cats and share a few quiet bonding minutes together.

When I got home at around 1 a.m., I didn't want to forget a single second of what had just happened. I opened my Voice Memos app and started recording myself, singing bits of the songs I'd just heard. Then I opened my Notes app, trying to document every detail I could remember from the entire experience. The next morning, I realized the chorus of "I Did Something Bad" had made its way into my dreams. I always knew there was a witchy spell in that song.

People often say, "Never meet your heroes," the idea being that they'll never live up to the version of them you've built in your head. But that day proved the opposite. Taylor was sincere, gracious, and somehow managed to exceed every hope and expectation I'd ever had. As soon as I posted the beach chair photo of us on my personal Instagram account, I went over to Tumblr, shared a screenshot of it, and thanked Taylor for such an incredible night, adding a little note asking her if she could go give it a like. A few minutes later, she did just that, once again showing how much she cared about the little things that meant everything to us. After that day, I changed my @swiftiesforeternity Instagram profile photo—and I haven't touched it since.

Everything Has Changed

In 2023, at twenty-two, I was working my first corporate job out of college in Nashville, Tennessee—ironically, at a book publishing company. I managed their social media accounts and helped with publicity and marketing. But in late April, I was laid off due to budget cuts. Soon after, my soul dog, Belle, passed away. She had been by my side for nearly eighteen years, and losing her felt like the world had shifted beneath me. It was undeniably the worst summer of my life. I found myself completely unanchored, unsure of where I was headed.

But as they say, "Everything happens for a reason," and in my case the timing couldn't have been more serendipitous. Thanks to the Eras Tour, my Instagram account, @swiftiesforeternity, started gaining serious traction, and with the support of this community, I was able to make social media my full-time job. Through it, I've connected with people I never would've met if it weren't for our shared passion for Taylor and her music. My account essentially became *LinkedIn (Taylor's Version)*. During the lead-up to *The Tortured Poets Department* album, I was contacted by outlets like CNN, invited to do radio interviews, and featured on several podcasts—including one hosted by Barstool Sports. Suddenly, new doors began flying open.

In the fall of 2024, life took another turn. I found myself in a dreamlike whirlwind, going to Kansas City Chiefs games and award shows on what felt like a near-weekly basis, all of which became part of my social media content. Through it all, I met some of the most inspiring people, traveled solo, stepped far outside my comfort zone, learned hard lessons, and grew immensely, both personally and professionally.

One night, I was at the 2025 AFC Championship Game, a nail-biter that could've gone either way. I had quickly learned that this was the way with the Chiefs, as they almost always pulled through at the very last second. When the win finally came, the whole room burst into applause and embraces, strangers celebrating like lifelong friends. Taylor was high-fiving everyone as we all moved toward the field, swept up in the joy. Somewhere between the tunnel and the turf, it struck me how extraordinary it all was—that what began as a love for her music had carried me to places I never could have imagined, even football fields. As confetti rained down, I stood there in awe, knowing I was living a full-circle moment I'd hold on to forever.

Forever & Always

For me, being a Swiftie has never just existed online. It's been a part of my real, everyday life for as long as I can remember—and I remember it *all too well*. When I was a freshman in high school, I felt oddly proud that I could finally relate to the lyrics in "Fifteen." On days when friends disappointed me, my mom and I would go out instead, blasting Taylor's music through the car speakers as if the songs had been written just for us. Back then I'd post photos, videos, and spontaneous thoughts of mine on Tumblr, hoping that someday Taylor might notice. I'd sit in class, letting her lyrics carry me away as I imagined little stories of my own. I often wondered if anyone else did the same—if they, too, saw themselves in the words of someone they'd never met.

Eventually, I found those people. They weren't the friends from school lunch tables or Friday-night plans—they were scattered across the internet, embedded in a fan community that ran deeper than most could comprehend. While my peers were busy with whatever else teenagers were "supposed" to care about, I was investing my time in people who felt poetry in their core. Those who understood what it meant to be a Taylor Swift fan—that it was extremely personal, transformative, and powerful in a way that remained long after the music stopped. At the time, some of my friendships lived entirely in Instagram DMs, bound by midnight album countdowns and a mutual appreciation for the same artist.

Soon we turned those digital bonds into real-world memories. We booked flights and met up in cities we'd never been to. We road-tripped across state lines to attend as many shows as we could. We danced barefoot at the back of stadium floors where there was space to spin in circles. We cracked secret codes: racing to the barricade before Taylor walked by, sneaking our friends onto the floor, and dancing our hearts out, hoping Andrea might notice and choose us for that once-in-a-lifetime chance to meet Taylor after the show. It felt like being part of a high-spirit rebellion—like a secret summer camp just for us, where familiar faces from profile pictures and usernames came to life in hotel lobbies and merch lines.

Through it all, it always seemed like Taylor was in on the magic with us, like when she walked by the barricade and recognized a group of us who had once been invited to her home for a Secret Session. Or the times she left comments on fans' posts during their lowest moments, reminding them that everything would be okay. The Swiftie community became what it is today because of the way she made us feel—not like customers, but like friends. It was never transactional. We were never just the people who bought her music. We were the most important part of her story. Even during challenging times, when she stepped away from the spotlight, she never made it about just her struggle. Instead, she said *we* went through it, because she knew that when life got hard for her, it affected all of us too. Not in the same way, of course, but in that unique way that comes from loving and believing in someone who's so often misunderstood by those outside the fandom. We stood up for her when she shouldn't have needed defending, but it was the least we could do. She has given us so much—a space for our emotions to live, moments to hold close, strength to move forward, and someone to look up to. It was our way of saying thank you.

Our story isn't confined to a single experience of being a fan or running a fan account. It's about the many layers of what it truly means to be a Swiftie—the lyrics that shaped us, the late-night drives where her songs brought us clarity, the eighty thousand voices echoing in stadiums like one unified chorus. But it's also about the ones who were there in the early days, lining up at mall tours and fairgrounds, holding handmade signs and the hope that they were witnessing a future *superstar*. It's the kitchen dance parties, the friendships deepened by a mutual passion, and the memories we'll carry with us—the ones that, one day, will *break our fall.* This is a celebration of everything that makes us more than just a fandom. It's a lifelong bond, a source of comfort, and a reminder that no matter where we come from, we're part of something bigger. This is a tribute to our story. A rare kind of love and community that comes around only *once every few lifetimes.* And somehow, it still feels like we're just getting started.

Next Chapter

Junior Jewels

CHAPTER TWO

The Music

For most of us, it began with a song. A lyric that struck a chord so deep, we had to know more about the girl who wrote it. Whether you've been here since the first era or joined our journey a few albums in, you've likely fallen in love with every part of her discography. And when life feels a little too still or a little too overwhelming—when you realize you really are *on your own, kid*—there's always been a Taylor Swift song waiting to meet you there. To say the words you couldn't find. To speak the feelings you didn't know how to name. To remind you that you're not alone.

Taylor's Music Is Our Own Time Capsule

We often think of Taylor's albums as a way to revisit the past. Whether it's reliving a happy memory or remembering a difficult chapter, her songs hold emotions that remain relevant no matter how much time has passed. Many of her tracks, if not all, are ones we return to throughout our lives, discovering new layers of meaning as we grow. Sometimes, you find yourself connecting with a song in a completely different, more grown-up kind of way.

That's something many of us particularly felt with the re-recordings. The *Taylor's Version* albums gave us the chance to reconnect with the music we've always loved, not just in a nostalgic way but from an entirely new perspective. These re-releases created space for us to meet our younger selves with kindness, while also appreciating how far we've come. Our relationship with her albums may evolve over time, but our affinity for them doesn't fade—it deepens. In fact, the re-recordings are proof of something I've always known: Taylor Swift's music is *timeless*.

In my opinion, a Taylor Swift album is as close as you could get to time traveling. Hearing "I was riding shotgun with my hair undone in the front seat of his car" whisks me back to my childhood room, blasting "Our Song" and screaming along as if I could relate at eight years old. "Fearless" sweeps me into the time I daydreamed about my first kiss. "Better Than Revenge" brings back memories of the girl who stole my middle-school boyfriend—though, like Taylor, I've learned that no one can truly take someone who doesn't want to leave. "We Are Never Ever Getting Back Together" plays on the radio, and I'm reminded of the last time I officially ended things with someone I knew didn't deserve my energy.

The intro of "Welcome To New York" carries me to my freshman year college dorm, feeling like the world was mine to conquer. The entire *reputation* album takes me back to sitting in Taylor's living room with my mom, hearing it for the first time, knowing it was a moment I had unknowingly longed for. *Folklore* and *evermore* transport me to the idealistic worlds I escaped to during the harsh realities of living through a global pandemic in 2020. *Midnights* reminds me of graduating college and realizing, for the first time ever, that I was truly on my own—living in a new city, far from everything and everyone that once felt familiar. And *The Tortured Poets Department* brings me to the most thrilling, chaotic chapter the fandom has ever known, but also to a time when I finally felt I understood my *place in this world*.

Taylor's music has become so intertwined with our own stories that, with the click of a button, we're able to relive them all. It's like opening a diary filled with old personal journal entries. You'll cringe, you'll smile, you'll cry, and you'll heal. But no matter what, you know you will feel.

So let's rewind the clock and revisit each era that brought us here.

First, open your closet, dust off your old cowboy boots—we're stepping into the Debut era. This era is all about a thick Southern accent, blue jeans, pickup trucks, teardrops on a guitar, and the raw sparkle of wide-eyed dreams. It's the true beginning of our story. To us, the *Taylor Swift* album radiates pure, unfiltered naivete: the kind of childlike innocence you wish you could preserve forever. It feels like slipping on brand-new cowboy boots. They're pristine: shiny, stiff, and full of promise. While you may desperately want to keep them that way, each song on this album is like taking another step, and once you start walking, the leather softens. Scuff marks appear. Six months later, they're worn-in and weathered, covered in scratches and scrapes you once tried to avoid. But now? You see the beauty in them. They hold the proof that you've started living—with all the highs and the lows that come along the way. And just like those boots, you're better equipped for the long road ahead.

You're in high school now, daydreaming about running off with someone your parents would definitely disapprove of. You haven't quite let go of those cowboy boots, but you've now added a ballgown to the mix. Welcome to *Fearless*, where fairy tales and teenage rebellion exist in the same breath. If we had to pick one word to define this era, it would be "*passion*." Everything is felt with such force—the love, the heartbreak, the anger, the fear, the dreaming. Subtlety simply doesn't live here. This is an era of extremes, where emotions hit hard and often, and that's exactly what makes it unforgettable. We've all lived through our own teenage storms, which is why songs like "You're Not Sorry" and "You Belong With Me" hit so close to home. The longing. The frustration. The hope that maybe, just maybe, love will conquer all. It's about chasing that rush—the kind that makes your heart race anytime you're around someone new, or when you're dancing in the pouring rain in a brand-new dress, not even caring as it clings to your skin. In that fleeting moment, you feel fully alive. Gold sequins, hand hearts, messy curls, and fearless declarations became hallmarks of this era. But being fearless doesn't mean you're not afraid; rather, you are and you leap anyway. This is the era where you learn that even if you *fall*, it was still worth the *jump*.

It's time to grab your wedding attire, we're crashing a ceremony. This is the *Speak Now* era, where emotions run high, enchanting stories get messy, and love sometimes shows up uninvited. Have you ever felt the urge to boldly declare your heart before it's too late? That's the spirit of this soundtrack. It's an ode to those of us who wear our hearts on our sleeves—the ones who fall fast, love fiercely, and hurt easily. It encapsulates the bittersweet innocence of youth—when romance feels effortless, flawless, and eternal, yet leaves us blind to the heartbreaks waiting just around the corner. More than the pain, *Speak Now* is about transformation: the second we shed that fragile innocence and discover that the real beauty lies in being unapologetically honest about our feelings, regardless of how the story may unfold. And perhaps most importantly, this era celebrates the enduring legacy of the Swiftie kingdom Taylor has forged alongside us. "Long Live" remains our shared anthem, a song that binds us through every era to come. Nearly two decades later, we are still moving mountains together, our crowns still intact.

Reach into your drawer and pull out that old, forgotten scarf. We're entering the *Red* era. Ask any of us what this album represents, and you'll likely get the same response. For us, *Red* is the unmistakable sign that autumn has arrived. It feels like a brisk walk on a chilly morning, leaves crunching beneath your feet with each step. Everything starts to shift: Knee-high socks are pulled up, mittens and scarves reappear, and life looks a little more colorful. But it's so much more than just a seasonal soundtrack or a perfectly curated Pinterest board. *Red* is a full sensory experience. If this album were a person, it would be that free-spirited being you can't help but admire—the one who is carefree and radiant, dancing barefoot in the kitchen at midnight but crying in the taxi home, because their ability to feel those exhilarating highs also means they feel the crushing lows just as profoundly. It's "22" when you're in love with life, singing with friends at your birthday party, convinced the world is full of endless possibility. But it's also "The Moment I Knew," when your heart shatters in real time because that one person didn't show up when it mattered most. *Red* doesn't just color your world; it stains it like lipstick, in every shade of love and heartbreak. This album is our biggest, coziest blanket when life feels chaotic and unpredictable—a warm refuge where all those tangled feelings can finally live and breathe.

Pick up your Polaroid camera and keep that red lipstick on—we're heading back to *1989*. This is your move-to-a-new-city, start-over, self-discovery era. The skyline glows with promise, and every moment is filled with excitement. This time, the romanticization isn't just about a person. It's about a place. New York City is the heartbeat of this album. From the opening notes of "Welcome To New York," this shimmering synth-pop record channels the thrill of stepping into your own power, of chasing freedom, and embracing the unknown. It's the realization that no one really has it all figured out, and that's exactly what makes life so beautiful. If you've ever moved somewhere new on your own, these songs became your soundtrack. They mark one of life's most pivotal seasons: adulthood in full bloom, and with high-waisted shorts, skirts, crop tops, and a bob, the style of this era was defining. The *1989* album holds the stories you'll one day share with your kids—tales of firsts and farewells, of missteps and milestones, and the spontaneous, messy escapades that led you to finding yourself. And somehow, *it was everything*.

Slide on your snake rings, lace up your combat boots, and step boldly into the *reputation* era—a realm where strength and fragility collide, and where revenge and glitter exist side by side. We've all felt misunderstood at some point. Sometimes it's by our parents, our friends, our partners, or even the world itself. In Taylor's case, it was the world. That's why it's fitting, and a little ironic, that *reputation* became her most misunderstood album. To outsiders, it might seem shadowed and bitter. But to us, it's a story of reclamation, resilience, and rebirth. This album lives in duality. It opens with ". . . Ready For It?," venomous and defiant, a track that seizes control and demands attention, and closes with the gentle intimacy of "New Year's Day." If you're walking through a storm of your own, this track list reminds you that light can still find its way in, if you let it. Happiness can shine even through sadness, and rising from the ashes is part of life's odyssey. More than anything, *reputation* is about refusing to let anyone else define you. Your power comes from owning your story—even the parts people try to use against you. As much as we wish it were, life isn't always soft and easy. It's not always rainbows and butterflies. Sometimes, you might get a few snakes.

Shedding our snake skin, we reach for our pastel journal and rose-colored glasses. You'll need both as we enter the *Lover* era—one actually full of rainbows and butterflies. This is the calm after the storm. At first glance, the album looks like a celebration of love—I mean, it's in the title, after all. But beneath the sweetness lies something far more intricate: the vulnerability that comes with learning to trust again in the wake of betrayal.

These songs shimmer with golden warmth, yet hum quietly with the kind of anxiety that only comes from caring so deeply that it might undo you if it ever fell apart. This is the heart-shaped vinyl you spin when you're so wildly in love that you'd marry them with *paper rings*. However, it's also the one you reach for when you're haunted by the insecurities you've tried so hard to bury. Cue "The Archer." You find yourself wondering if the person you care for so much might one day leave, because why wouldn't they? You hear those same doubts in "Cornelia Street," where the fear of loss lingers in every lyric. Yet you feel the complete opposite in "Lover," where for once, forever seems within reach.

This album saves us a seat at love's table, right beside its contradictions—where it can be both tender and terrifying, fierce and fragile. Still, we choose to stay, holding our breath and hoping this time, your *lover* will choose to stay too.

Go under your bed, find your cardigan collection, and pick your favorite—because we've officially entered the *folkmore* era. *Folklore* and *evermore* are two sides of the same coin: One is airy and searching, reaching for fleeting glimpses of light and living for the hope of it all, while the other is colder and introspective and feels like the hushed intimacy of winter evenings. Together, they create a world just far enough from reality, where you can disappear into the woods to be alone or daydream on a sun-drenched August beach day, hoping to be found by that one special person. These sister albums offer more than just escapism. They are the flicker of candlelight in a secluded cabin. The rustle of willow trees. The reflection of a mirrorball in an empty room. The pop of a champagne bottle. The salt in the air of your treasured summer beach town. The nostalgia of returning home for holidays. These are the stories we tell around a campfire in the woods, glass of red wine in hand and friends all around. The stories of love triangles, grief, and what could have been. *Folklore* and *evermore* aren't just albums. They're an atmosphere. A cinematic universe. A state of mind. They taught us that even in fiction, the feelings are real. And sometimes, the stories we invent are the ones that reveal our truths the most.

As dusk settles over the world of *folkmore*, night begins to fall. When the clock strikes midnight and the rest of the world is asleep, with the moon and stars above, that's when your mind starts to wander. Have you ever found yourself wide awake at 3 a.m., caught in a web of endless thoughts? That restless, ruminative feeling is *Midnights*. Imagine yourself wrapped in a blanket, headphones gently resting over your ears, pressing play and being swept into a dreamlike journey through your memories. This album feels like flipping through the pages of an old diary, each track a snapshot of longing and late-night vulnerability. As you listen to songs like "Would've, Could've, Should've" and "Maroon," you may stumble upon emotions you thought you'd locked away—regrets you wish you could rewrite, recollections too precious to let go, moments you ache to relive. *Midnights* is wrapped in the imagery of the night sky, the ticking of clocks marking the passage of time, and mirrors reflecting who we were, who we are, and who we still could become.

The clock keeps turning back—this time, to an age of typewriters and ink pens. We're being admitted into *The Tortured Poets Department*. This is Taylor at her most literary, her most bruised, her most Shakespearean. The album is a chronicle of heartbreak and obsession, laced with tragedy and hyper self-awareness. We all know what it's like to put on a brave face while we're silently falling apart. You know, those times where you have no choice but to *fake it till you make it* at work, at school, or in life. "I Can Do It With a Broken Heart" becomes the anthem for holding it together, perfectly embodying that silent, stubborn strength it takes to keep moving forward even when everything hurts. This album pulls us into a raw, unfiltered *love story*—one filled with gaslighting, empty promises, and the emotional turbulence that makes you question it all. It's not the fairy-tale romance we once dreamed of. It's messy and painful, yet dangerously magnetic. This era feels like a shared confession, a community of "tortured poets" who wear their scars proudly. Taylor's songwriting on this album is some of her most mature and vulnerable to date. It reminds us that when you're in the thick of heartbreak, it can feel impossible to believe you'll ever make it out. You might feel like you're drowning, like the pain will never fade, like you're losing yourself completely. But with time, healing arrives in unexpected ways. On the other side of pain, there's growth. There's strength. There's hope—and more love waiting to be found.

The ink has dried, and now the curtains rise. No longer lost in the depths of heartbreak, you slip into your bright-orange showgirl outfit and step into the spotlight, ready to put on the performance of your life. *The Life of a Showgirl* is glamorous and theatrical, captivating us with dazzling lights and intoxicating melodies. It's also a love so confident it finally breaks down the walls you once thought would stand for all time. You can feel its truth; it is real, unshakable, unbreakable. Each track is a celebration of freedom and self-assurance, a playful flirtation with the risqué—Taylor's witty double entendres, like in "Wood," make mischief feel effortless—and a reminder of the simple pleasures of life beyond the stage. The title track, "The Life of a Showgirl," hints at the sacrifices hidden beneath the glitter: long nights, relentless performances, the giving of oneself to the audience over and over again, and the toll it can take on your body and mind. Yet this is the life you chose. Despite the demands of the spotlight, the album radiates empowerment, sensuality, and, ultimately, *peace*. By the end of the show, we're no longer trapped by the past. We've been saved from our tower, *no longer drowning and deceived*, and freed from "The Fate of Ophelia," alive like never before.

Whether you're reflecting on your early years with Debut or *missing lovers past* with *Midnights*, we can all agree that Taylor's albums have been a guiding light—cathartic, steadfast, and there to carry us through life's firsts. There's the first time you fall in love, and the first time your heart breaks. The first time you find a best friend, and the first time you lose one. The first time you love someone unconditionally, and the first time you grieve someone you were never ready to lose. The first time everything goes exactly as planned, and the first time it all unravels without warning. I could list a hundred more, but you get the idea . . . there's a song for it all. As we try to make sense of life, Taylor's music gives us the words to express our own emotions—often saying what we cannot. It's no wonder her music resonates so powerfully.

The Art of Courage

Fearless may be one of Taylor's album titles, but it's also a thread that runs through everything she's ever created, showing itself in her willingness to share her most intimate thoughts with the world, even knowing they might be picked apart, misinterpreted, or judged by those who don't really know her. I can only imagine how daunting and fear-inducing that must be, especially when you start opening up at such a young age. However, over time, she's mastered the balance and learned how to play the game. You don't gain that kind of resilience without being dragged through the mud a few times.

With every song, she encouraged us to own our feelings unapologetically, leaving no room for anyone else to invalidate them. If she could rise above the whispers of hate and keep shining, then there's no reason we can't do the same. Taylor has modeled this bravery since her very first album, and each era since has become a lesson in itself: owning your name, risking everything in pursuit of something that lasts, speaking up when something matters, loving someone in the face of uncertainty, finding joy in your single era, reclaiming your reputation when others try to destroy it, giving your heart away again, escaping into art when the real world feels too heavy, revisiting pivotal moments from your past, performing through your biggest heartbreak, and choosing your own happiness. While we all have the chance to be courageous in our own lives, her songs remind us that it's not fear itself that defines us, but rather how we choose to face it.

Do you dive in headfirst?

Taylor does. And she does it *fearlessly*.

The Depth Is in the Details

Entertainment is one of the most powerful forms of art, offering an escape from the turmoil in our minds. I appreciate all kinds of art, but there's something uniquely therapeutic about music. For me, it's been a source of safety in more ways than I can count. The lyrics and sound come together to create a kind of sonic therapy. Over the years, I've connected with many different artists. Some albums stay with me for just a little while, tied to a specific season of my life, while others become part of who I am. As you might have guessed, Taylor's albums fall into the category of being eternally etched into my soul. What sets Taylor apart from other artists is the intricate detail woven through her lyrics. You don't need to be the same age as her to find yourself in her songs. She distills universal human emotions, offering clarity and perspective no matter your amount of life experience.

There are countless songs about heartbreak that exist, but hers always speak to me the loudest. The metaphors, the imagery, and the almost-too-specific recounting she dares to include—details some might call insignificant—are exactly what make her writing so significant. That's why whether she's singing a pop anthem, leaning in to rock and roll, or sitting alone with just her guitar, we find ourselves enamored by all of it. Her production is masterful, yes—but what truly draws us in is everything hidden beneath the surface. In Taylor's art, the little things are the big things.

It's the heartbeat fading to a flatline in "You're Losing Me," the double entendres tucked inside deceptively simple lyrics and the anxiety-induced, rapid-fire pacing of "So Long, London." It's sampling her own background vocals from "Out Of the Woods" in "Question . . . ?," allowing past versions of herself to echo into the present. It's including her late grandmother's vocals in "marjorie," not just to honor her legacy but to let her voice finally be heard in stadiums, fulfilling her grandmother's dream. Then there are the emotional callbacks entwined between songs like themes in a series of novels. The teenage love triangle between Betty, August, and James is a prime example of storytelling through interconnected tracks. Even the timestamps align—at 2:47 in "betty," we hear "James, get in, let's drive"; at 2:47 in "august," "Get in the car." At 3:14 in "betty," "I'm here on your doorstep" mirrors the 3:14 line in "cardigan," "You'd be standing in my front porch light." Whether those timestamps were *all by design* or merely coincidence, we may never know. Still, it makes us feel like we've discovered secret passageways within her songwriting, each one leading us further into her universe.

Decoding the meaning behind Taylor's lyrics has always been one of our favorite pastimes. While yes, we're sometimes curious about what in her life inspired a certain line, more often we just want to understand the songs so we can glimpse the layers of her artistry—and of course, relate them back to our own stories. The true genius of her songwriting lies in the fact that even when you can't directly relate to a song's story, its poetic nature lets you slip into a version of yourself who can. You empathize, you envision, and you're entirely transported.

The Romanticization

We all watch rom-coms, right? I watch them because they make me believe in the things I once believed in as a kid—that we'll all find our person, and that life can be perfectly imperfect. Sure, they're also wildly entertaining, especially when you've got people like Matthew McConaughey and Kate Hudson lighting up the screen. But if there's one thing you probably already know about Swifties, it's that we're obsessed with romance. The idea of it, the feelings it stirs up, and everything that comes along with it. We're basically a collective of overthinking hopeless romantics searching for our own rom-com ending, including Taylor herself. It's almost like being a Swiftie comes with its own emotional horoscope: We romanticize everything. We'd even settle for the passionate rom-com arguments because they always lead back to more love. And I know I'm not alone when I say I tend to be drawn to Taylor's most heartbreaking songs—not because I enjoy sadness, but because I want to feel something that is real. As someone who has yet to experience falling in love, I'm fascinated by it. I want to feel that kind of devotion, the kind that aches when it's gone. There's something oddly comforting in heartbreak when it means you once had something worth missing that much. Sometimes, I wonder if that's just me, or if it's simply human nature—to crave *any* feeling, even pain, because it's better than feeling nothing at all. Maybe that's exactly why we connect to Taylor's music. Like so many, she idealized romance long before she ever lived it. Through her songs, we've found a way to do the same.

Listening to Taylor's stories—about falling in love, falling out of love, and everything in between—has resonated with us in a way that lets us feel our own emotions without guilt or shame. Her vulnerability validates ours. It reminds us that we're not dramatic or broken for having big feelings—we're simply human. If Taylor Swift can move through those messy, complicated feelings—build a happy, fulfilling life, and still find a love worthy of her, then maybe we can too.

Part of the reason we've been rooting for Taylor since she was fifteen is because, deep down, we've also been rooting for ourselves. We see pieces of ourselves in her story. Her wins feel like our wins. So when she entered a relationship that sparked a defining cultural movement, it wasn't solely about the romance of it all—it was about what it represented. After nearly two decades of navigating the highs and lows of relationships together, it felt like she was finally being seen, celebrated, and cherished in the way we'd always hoped she would be. Just like we hope to one day be ourselves. It felt, quite literally, like "If This Was A Movie": the global pop powerhouse and the star athlete on the world stage. No matter what happens in her life, we know she'll keep writing, we'll keep listening, and the songs, regardless of what inspired them, will continue to evolve with us, taking on new meanings long after the moment has passed.

The Power of Connection

Arguably, the most essential part of the human experience is connection. We all crave it. It's what makes intimacy possible and helps loneliness fade away. When I meet another Swiftie, I know the words that helped them through hard times are the same ones that helped me through mine. The lyrics that made them spin and dance around in their bedrooms are the same ones I danced to. Taylor's music creates real human connection across *the land, the sea, and the sky*.

When I was in high school, I had friends across different crowds, but I never felt fully accepted by any one group. I was a solo act, floating between circles but doing my own thing: playing sports, listening to Taylor's music, exploring my own niche interests. Still, the social hierarchy got to me at times. I remember thinking how much easier life would be if I were the prettiest, most popular girl in school—the one all the boys swooned over. At that age, social status felt paramount. Then I'd listen to "Fifteen," and I'd be reminded that my teen years might not be what I expected, but it was only such a small chapter of my life, and I was destined for *things greater than dating the boy on the football team* (or, in Taylor's case, you might do both). Hearing that from someone I looked up to so much not only made me, and millions like me, feel understood in those awkward, angst-filled teenage years but also gave us the hope we needed to keep looking forward.

I found comfort in the fact that Taylor had never been the "it girl" either. She was unique, which isn't always celebrated when you're young. But instead of shrinking herself to blend in, she turned her individuality into her superpower. Now undoubtedly one of the most famous women in the world, she has become the ultimate proof that popularity holds no worth once you reach adulthood. Embracing her authentic self didn't just become part of her success story—it became part of her brand. She's spoken openly about that outsider feeling over the years. As she once told *Vogue*: "I don't ever feel like the cool kid at the party, ever. It's like, Smile and be nice to everybody, because you were not invited to be here . . . All of my favorite people—people I really trust—none of them were cool in their younger years." Taylor channeled her struggles into songs that gave even the so-called cool people who secretly felt the same way a place to belong. From "The Outside," a raw anthem about feeling like an outcast, to "The Best Day," a tender reflection of finding safety in family, she used songwriting as a way to fill a void. And even when she wasn't writing about herself, she found escape in imagining other people's stories.

"Mary's Song (Oh My My My)," inspired by a neighbor's lifelong love story, wasn't her experience, but it was a version of love she chose to believe in—and invited us to believe in too. Whether through her own life or someone else's, she was always building dreamlands we could run to.

"PEOPLE HAVEN'T ALWAYS BEEN THERE FOR ME, BUT MUSIC ALWAYS HAS." - TS

You know how people always say journaling helps because writing your thoughts down can release bottled-up emotions? The truth is, sometimes I'm too tired or overwhelmed to even try. My mind gets so cluttered, I wouldn't even know where to begin. Instead, I turn on a Taylor Swift song. Somehow, she's already written down everything I feel. The way she captures and untangles emotions I haven't fully processed makes me feel lighter—like I've just poured my heart out on the page. In the midst of so much noise, her music has always been my place of peace.

Taylor often says her songs may have started out being about her life, but now they're about ours. During one of her Eras Tour stops, she stated:

> *I've been playing shows sort of as a coping mechanism my whole life. . . . I go through this process where I feel a thing, I write a song about that thing, I show it to you, and I go, "Do you like it? Did you ever feel this way too . . . ?" And so,*

> *you know, when you guys are at a show, and you . . . I mean, if you even nod your head or make eye contact with me or sing the words to a song during a show, that to me validates that emotion and makes me feel like I wasn't alone in feeling it.*

That's exactly what she gives us in return. Being on this twenty-year journey with her feels like we're in the twentieth season of a hit TV show we just can't stop watching. Fittingly, we'd even have the perfect title for it—personally approved by our chairman: *Female Rage: The Musical*.

People often ask why we are so invested in Taylor's life's journey. It's because we've grown up alongside her. We've experienced life with her: love and loss, heartbreak and healing, friendship and loneliness, loyalty and betrayal, pleasure and pain, trauma and triumph. Whenever we've felt lost or isolated, wishing someone could truly see and understand us, her music reached out and took our hand. Her words have always felt like a best friend whispering, "I get it. You're not alone. You're not crazy. I've been there too. You'll be okay. I'm here for you." I'm not exaggerating when I say this, and I know I'm not alone: I wouldn't be the person I am today without Taylor's music and the people it's brought into my life. Through her music, and through those who understand it as I do, I've found my safe haven. Isn't it beautiful to think that we're all tied together by *an invisible string*, woven from friendship bracelets and decades of shared eras—simply because one remarkable person chose to share her gift with the world?

RECIPES
COOKIES
BREAD
REP
SWIFTMAS

CHAPTER THREE

The Parasocial Relationship Is Mutual, I Promise

As a Swiftie, odds are you've heard the term "parasocial" before. You know, that feeling of having a one-sided connection with someone you've never met. In fact, in 2025, *parasocial* was Cambridge Dictionary's Word of the Year, and Swifties were largely credited for it. Most of us are fully aware that our relationship with Taylor falls into that category—we feel like we know her, even if we've met her only once or not at all. Though, we're not completely delusional. At least, most of us aren't. We understand she's a celebrity who chooses what parts of her life to share. That said, the connection we feel isn't entirely one-sided. In fact, it's what this entire fandom was built on. From the very beginning, when she had just a handful of fans, Taylor went out of her way to make us feel valued and appreciated. And as her fame grew, she never stopped. She kept interacting with us online, showing up unexpectedly, hosting Secret Sessions, and meeting as many of us as humanly possible. So when people talk about the "Swiftie effect," they need to understand that it didn't happen by happenstance. This loyalty, this fierce devotion, is rooted in how she has always shown up for us. That's what sets her apart. She's not just a pop star we admire from afar. She's someone who, in her own way, has let us into her life. Whether it's through the honesty of her lyrics, a reply on Tumblr, or an invitation into her home, she's built a relationship with us that goes far beyond the typical artist-fan dynamic. And that's why we don't just support her music; we support her as a person too.

The Start of an Age

Since 2006, Taylor has nurtured her connection with us. In 2010, when she was just twenty years old and nearing the end of her *Fearless* Tour, she hosted an all-day meet and greet with Swifties in Nashville. Over two thousand people showed up, many of them waiting more than twenty-four hours for the chance to meet her. To make sure they weren't just sitting around bored, Taylor had her team set up interactive experiences throughout the building—meet and greets with her band members, tours of her buses, makeup stations, greeting card booths, and more. While fans took part in these activities—or walked the halls singing Taylor's songs in hopes of being noticed—her team would go around randomly selecting the most passionate ones to meet her. Of course, since the Swifties weren't getting breaks, she decided she wouldn't either. She stood there for thirteen hours straight, meeting fans one by one, never rushing the moment, a day that would go on to define how our fan-artist relationship would continue to evolve over the years.

Not even a year later, in 2011, Taylor was already on her second world tour for her album *Speak Now*. By writing the entire album on her own, not only had she solidified her place in the music industry and earned massive respect from her peers, but her music reached more listeners, and the fan base flourished. As our community grew, so did our bond.

In May of that same year, a soon-to-be-four-year-old boy named Ronan passed away from neuroblastoma. His mother, Maya Thompson, had been writing a blog called *Rockstar Ronan*, documenting his nine-month battle with cancer in an effort to raise awareness for childhood cancer causes. Even after Ronan's passing, she continued blogging about her grief, often writing letters to her son as if he were still alive. Later that year, in October, Taylor invited Maya to one of her shows and asked to meet her. She had been following Maya's blog and wanted to share that she had written a song inspired by Ronan's story. The song was titled "Ronan," but it wasn't just a tribute; Taylor had listed Maya as a cowriter on the track, with all proceeds going to childhood cancer charities. With Maya's permission, Taylor went on to perform the song for the first time at a Stand Up To Cancer show. To this day, they still keep in touch, and Taylor invites her to a show on every tour she embarks on.

That kind of intimacy with fans is something she's never lost—even as her fame catapulted to *new heights* with *1989*. The album was embraced around the globe, especially in places where pop music had long overshadowed country. It marked a turning point in her career, one that brought in millions of new Swifties and officially crowned her a global pop icon. As longtime supporters, we came to terms with the idea that she might now be *untouchable*. Gone was our favorite small-town country artist and in her place stood a formidable force of influence. Then Taylor did what she always does: She found new, meaningful ways to keep us all close.

The Other Side of the Door

Imagine Taylor Swift showing up at your house unannounced. Do you hesitate, or do you just open the door? In 2014, this happened to a Connecticut Swiftie named Stephanie Barnett. Not only did Taylor knock on her door, but she also brought gifts for Stephanie's toddler, Leyton . . . as if her presence alone wasn't already enough. For a fan, having your idol show up at your front door is beyond rare—it's a once-in-a-lifetime moment. Even though this was just one fan's experience, it felt like something we all lived together. Seeing someone's dream come true within our community made it feel more real for all of us. It made us wonder: *Maybe this could happen to me someday.* This wasn't the last time Taylor made a surprise visit to a fan's home; a few years later, she did the same in London. As for Leyton, their bond didn't end at the doorstep. Taylor continued to share sweet moments with him at future tour stops, including gifting him the "22" hat at one of the Eras Tour shows.

Now imagine *you're* the one showing up to Taylor Swift's house because she invited you. This was the magic of the Secret Sessions.

If you're a longtime fan, you probably know all about these. Starting in the *1989* era in October 2014, Taylor handpicked fans from social media and invited them into her homes in Rhode Island, New York, LA, Nashville, and London. Most of the time, she'd find Swifties on Tumblr, Twitter, or Instagram, and then send them a direct message, before having her team reach out with more details. Baking cookies, eating pizza, swapping stories, singing together, and listening to unreleased music were just a few of the things that made these gatherings impossible to forget.

Another one of the most memorable Swiftie stories comes from Gena Gabrielle, a lifelong fan whose relationship with Taylor perfectly illustrates why so many of us stay devoted to her beyond the artistry. Gena had met Taylor several times at earlier meet and greets, but she never imagined that one day, Taylor would accept an invitation to attend her bridal shower. In 2014, Taylor flew to Columbus, Ohio, to surprise Gena—and vlogged the entire experience. She brought a collection of thoughtful gifts, including a framed watercolor painting she made, signed "Swift" in the bottom right corner.

In the video Taylor later posted on YouTube, she included a sweet note:

"Dearest Gena, thank you for inviting me to your bridal shower... and for inviting me into your life. (Since 2007!!!)"

Just one day before Taylor's birthday that year, on December 12, 2014, Gena was invited to present her with the Billboard Woman of the Year award—a full-circle moment that beautifully reflected the genuine connection they had built over time. A line from Gena's speech has always stayed with me: "I found Taylor because of her music, but I've stayed with her because of her character."

Swiftmas

Christmas that year became Swiftmas. Taylor sent fans giant boxes in the mail, filled with gifts she'd personally shopped for based on what she thought each Swiftie would love for the holidays. Handmade candles, scarves, gift cards, antiques, and merch were just a few of the things fans unwrapped. Each box also included a long, handwritten letter from Taylor—thanking them for listening to her music and explaining why she chose those specific gifts. She even shared a video of herself wrapping the presents with her mom and preparing the packages to send out. In the video, Meredith sat proudly on one of the gifts while Olivia lovingly left tiny bite marks on the wrapping paper. "I'm sure that Michelle will really appreciate having holes in her presents," Taylor joked. Once the gifts were delivered, she lurked online to watch and reply to fan reaction videos, making the whole experience feel even more special.

Taylurking

Early the following year, Taylor began rehearsing for her upcoming *1989* World Tour. She was in her *Sex and the City* era, slaying the streets of New York City with impeccable style and fully thriving in her single girl chapter. But of course, she still made time to prioritize us. She sent fans handwritten "Happy Valentine's Day" letters, and on actual Valentine's Day, Taylor reached out to a girl named Sophie who happened to be visiting NYC with her family. Sophie had posted online about her trip, and because Taylor was always lurking, she saw it and messaged her, inviting them over for the day. They spent hours together baking, chatting, playing with the cats, taking photos, and singing songs. Not many people can say their idol spontaneously invited them over to their house for a holiday, or any day, for that matter. But with just one message and a few hours of her time, Taylor turned the dreams of one of her biggest fans into a reality. It's gestures like these that continue to set her apart from other artists, reminding us that no matter how cherished she becomes by the rest of the world, she's never forgotten that we're the reason she gets to live out her own *wildest dreams*.

It was more than just grand gestures. Taylor had a way of making the smallest interactions online feel larger than life. Sometimes it was a simple comment or response—like when a fan once posted a photo of herself looking sad with the caption "I feel like everybody hates me," and Taylor shot back, "I don't hate you. There's one. Theory disproved." Or when a fan said Taylor's new bangs made her look like an elf "in the ethereal *Lord of the Rings* gorgeous and heavenly sort of way," and Taylor replied: "If only you knew what a high compliment this is to me. 'Mythical elf/ Santa's helper at the toy factory' is my aesthetic goal and to have achieved it, even just in your eyes, has truly made that haircut worthwhile. Thank you." There was also a time when one fan wrote, "Wish me luck on my physics test Tuesday," and Taylor replied, "Good luck on your physics test Tuesday!! Wish me luck on my album release Monday :)" Moments like these weren't scripted or staged. They felt like genuine exchanges, the kind of back-and-forth you'd have with a friend sitting in the same room as you. The same friend who posts giddy lists each fall about her chai cookie recipe, wearing plaid and ankle boots, drawing little pictures on foggy windows, and her love for pumpkin spice.

Taylor often took the time to write long, thoughtful messages to fans who were navigating life's ups and downs. In 2014, a Swiftie named Caillou Pettis was being bullied at school. Right away, she expressed admiration for him, letting him know that the qualities that made him different were not flaws—they were the seeds of his greatest strengths. She wrote,

> "Hi pal. I was really shocked to hear you say that you'd been bullied because of your name because the first thing I thought when I saw it was, 'Caillou is such a cool name.' Honestly. I thought it was so cool because it's different, and herein lies our issue: You will always be criticized and teased and bullied for things that make you different, but usually those things will be what set you apart. The things that set you apart from the pack, the things that you once thought were your weaknesses will someday become your strengths. So if they say you're weird or annoying or strange or too this or not enough that, maybe it's because you threaten them. Maybe you threaten them because you're not the norm. And if you're not the norm, give yourself a standing ovation."

Next, Taylor turned to a message of self-acceptance, encouraging Caillou to set mental boundaries and reminding him that his worth is defined not by others, but by what he chooses to believe about himself. She explained,

> "I think you look great the way you are. No one has the right to criticize you for how your body looks, but they will. One thing I've learned from experiencing this exact kind of

> criticism is that no one else can label your body except for you. No one gets to have a place in your mind if they weren't invited there by you. So please do me this one favor: Don't let their ugly words into your beautiful mind."

Finally, she addressed Caillou's safety, reminding him that while bullying with words might not have a direct penalty, "*except karma*," no one is ever allowed to physically hurt him. She encouraged him to take action if he is assaulted, emphasizing that it is serious and should never be ignored. At the same time, she praised his courage for sharing his story online and reassured him that he was strong. She signed off with,

> "Proud of you, Caillou Pettis."

The Golden Age

The *1989* era was a special time for us in general. Selfie sticks were everywhere, viral social media challenges like the ALS Ice Bucket Challenge were taking over our feeds, and having internet on your phone was no longer a luxury but a necessity. Apps like Twitter, Instagram, and of course Tumblr were exploding, completely redefining what it meant to be in a fandom. Our timelines became endless streams of tour updates, memes, theories, and late-night conversations with fans we'd never met in person but instantly felt intertwined with. I was spending every day talking with hundreds, maybe thousands, of fans online I didn't know in real life. Perhaps the most important part of 2015? It was the year Taylor took us all on the *1989* World Tour.

I remember being in bed, scrolling through Twitter and Tumblr, trying to keep up with where she was on the set list. I had to be up at 6 a.m. for school, but that didn't stop me from virtually taking part in the concert. Livestreams weren't really a thing yet, but I was still keeping up with other fans, laughing at GIFs that went instantly viral, and staying awake until she finished the show and headed backstage. That's when Loft '89 came into play: a secret room behind the stage filled with fans who were handpicked during the concert by Taylor's mom, Andrea. She'd walk through the crowd, looking for people having the most fun, wearing creative costumes, or sometimes even tracking down specific fans from Tumblr that Taylor wanted to meet. It was like a golden ticket moment. Fans I knew online were constantly changing their profile pictures to photos of themselves and Taylor.

After Loft '89, Taylor would often head to Tumblr to re-blog posts about that night's show, sometimes checking how fans she had met were reacting. So many inside jokes were born in those early Tumblr days. It truly felt like our own little slice of the internet. Unlike Instagram or Twitter, where hate and negativity could spread quickly, Tumblr felt safe and close-knit, like a giant virtual sleepover with just us and Taylor. Similarly to other Swifties, my biggest goal as a teenager wasn't to have a million friends or be invited to every party. I had a small circle and also my family, which was enough. What I really cared about was catching Taylor's attention on Tumblr. I spent so much of that year pouring my heart into posts, hoping she might see one, follow me, or maybe even want to meet me someday.

We would go to extreme lengths to get her attention on Tumblr. The feed was full of (now very cringeworthy) videos of us singing in our bedrooms, dancing on tables, and dramatically feeling every lyric as if we were living out our own music video. In true parasocial fashion, we were hopeful—no, convinced—that if Taylor just saw our post, she might comment or follow us. And because she actually did interact with us, we only doubled down, sometimes probably a little too aggressively. You see, Tumblr had a re-blogging feature that let you repost your own content as many times as you wanted, which meant the post would reappear in all your followers' feeds as if it were a brand-new one. Needless to say, we certainly abused it. Our dashboards were flooded with the same posts on repeat, especially if we knew she was online and Taylurking. I have no doubt she saw the same videos, photo edits, etc., time and time again. An account known as @taylornoticed kept meticulous track of every like, comment, or re-blog from Taylor, posting updates immediately after she interacted with one of us.

Then there were the other little quirks that defined the era. Like how every Swiftie's bio was akin to a trophy case: "Taylor liked 11x" or "Taylor followed on 12/13/15." Fans hoarded Taylor-inspired Tumblr usernames just to secure the best ones, and after the Secret Sessions, we were all frantically trying to remember lyrics from unreleased songs so we could claim them before anyone else. It sounds silly now, but back then those small things meant a lot to us.

To this day, every former Tumblr Swiftie likely still gets chills hearing the name IsTayOnTumblr.com—a website we all had on auto-refresh, waiting for it to say: "Taylor Swift liked a post

2 minutes ago." This meant it was time to go on a re-blogging spree. People in our real lives often rolled their eyes. "She's never going to notice you," they'd say. But we knew better. Because she did.

On August 17, 2015, it finally happened to me, and I saw the notification I had been waiting for: "taylorswift started following you." I was speechless. At fifteen, it felt like I had just peaked in life. Looking back now, I realize it was only the beginning.

She Rose Up from the Dead, She Does It All the Time

Fast-forward to 2017: Taylor Swift was still a household name, but that didn't stop anyone from canceling her the second they had the chance. To us, none of it mattered. We had been there when she rose up in 2006, and we were going to be here when she was ready to rise again. This time, it was our turn to remind her that she was appreciated, loved, and supported, no matter what.

When she returned, everything was different. Her resurgence wasn't to win back public favor or reclaim her title as America's sweetheart. She didn't do press interviews or traditional promo for her new album, *reputation*, because in her own words, there would be *no explanation, only reputation*. Instead, she trusted that the fans who knew her heart would still be there, and she was right. Her grand return wasn't on a red carpet or a magazine shoot; it was something far more intimate. In fact, it wasn't for the cameras at all. It was just her, a glass of white wine, her family, and a handful of her most loyal fans gathered in her living room, talking about life and music.

Taylor's generosity didn't stop at opening her home. It extended discreetly and compassionately into the real lives of those of us in need. In 2019, Ayesha Khurram was a fan struggling to pay for college. Her parents worked minimum-wage jobs, and her mom was overwhelmed with medical bills. After Ayesha posted online about potentially not being able to finish school, something incredible happened: Within two hours, she received a payment from Taylor Swift covering her outstanding tuition balance. The note read, "Ayesha, get your learn on, girl. I love you!" And just like that, her life was changed—all because of her favorite artist. This wasn't an isolated gesture. It was one of many times Taylor stepped in to help fans with tuition, rent, medical bills, or other financial hardships. Those brave enough to share their struggles online often found themselves unexpectedly supported by the very person whose music had already helped them through so much. At a time when many celebrities kept their distance, Taylor made intimacy her signature. We would always stand as *the moon to her Saturn*.

Baby, Just Say "Yes"

Over the years, Taylor has been more than a healing, almost therapeutic presence in our lives. She's even been the guest star at some of our biggest milestones! From weddings to engagements, she's found ways to make our love stories even more *dazzling*.

Picture this: You're celebrating your wedding day, and your favorite artist crashes it—she shows up unannounced, sings for you, and then parties with you and your family and friends. It sounds like a movie, but for Taylor Swift fans, it was real life. In 2016, that's exactly what happened. It turns out, Taylor had been in touch with the groom's sister, Ali, to plan the surprise. Ali shared that their mother had recently passed away, and that her brother and his now wife had gotten married by their mother's bedside in the hospital. On that day, the mother and son even had their first dance to "Blank Space" before she passed. Not only did Taylor sing the song during their official wedding ceremony but she also hand-painted a gift for the couple: a beautiful keepsake featuring the song's lyrics and the date of their special day. A few years later, she surprised another fan, Alex Goldschmidt, by singing "King Of My Heart" at his engagement party. If you're curious, there's a video on YouTube, and it's absolutely worth watching.

For You, Because of You

By 2021, Taylor had released her first re-recorded album, *Red (Taylor's Version)*. It was another defining moment in her career, but it didn't just ignite nostalgia for longtime fans; it also brought new ones into the fold. To celebrate the album's release, Taylor hosted a New York City premiere for *All Too Well: The Short Film*. She rented out an entire movie theater and, once again, handpicked fans from online to join her at the screening and celebrate its release.

The next premiere Taylor hosted came in 2023, for the highly anticipated *Taylor Swift: The Eras Tour* film in Los Angeles. By this point in her career, amid the most historic tour of all time, it was safe to say she was no longer just a pop star. She was now the most famous person on the planet. In 2023, she was the most Google-searched celebrity. You'd think that, at that level of fame, she'd have little time or energy to meet us, especially when it felt like the entire world was now one big Swiftie. But, true to form, Taylor still found a way. A typical film premiere might center around influencers, industry insiders, and A-list celebrities. However, nothing Taylor does is ever typical. That night, she spent time going fan by fan, personally meeting every single Swiftie she had invited, a scene reminiscent of that thirteen-hour meet and greet she once held. When it came time to watch the film, she didn't slip away to a private room; instead, she joined her fans, sitting in the theater surrounded by the very people who had made it all possible.

As things have evolved, and for good reason, Taylor has withdrawn from social media, aside from the occasional scroll through her favorite sourdough blogs. Yet she still finds ways to listen to us and keep a pulse on the fandom, likely with the help of her team and the sporadic posts friends and family send her. It's her way of staying a part of it, rather than above it. When Swifties joked that we wanted "more Lana" in "Snow On The Beach," she gave it to us. When we dreamed of hearing certain mash-ups live, she delivered them. Sometimes, that parasocial dynamic can go too far. And when it does, Taylor has no problem pushing back. The "But Daddy I Love Him" bridge is her reminder to everybody, fans included, that no one gets to dictate her life choices, no matter how close the connection may feel.

I could go on forever about our beautifully unique, slightly parasocial relationship with Taylor Swift. And I'm sure you could too, because truthfully, the events I've shared so far barely scratch the surface. For nearly two decades, she's been there for us in ways big and small—surprise visits, handwritten notes, meaningful gifts, invitations into her home and to her film premieres. When one of us runs into her, she's often the first to ask for a photo, which brings to mind what she once said—that she'd never tire of those encounters, because they were exactly what she had wished for as a little girl. It's in gestures like these that you see how she's never taken us for granted, always choosing to make us feel like friends. The best part of this fandom is that, just like Taylor does in her songs, we've turned the little things into the big things. The tiny jokes, the quick-witted comments, the inside references that lived on Tumblr—they've become just as defining as the rest of our story.

You Throw Your Head Back Laughing

Over the years, countless little interactions have snowballed into inside jokes, traditions, and fandom lore. It's worth pausing to revisit a few moments that have become part of our collective memory as a fandom.

1. No It's Becky

This is my personal favorite. What started as a bizarre internet post quickly turned into the most beloved joke among Swifties. Years ago, a Tumblr user posted a photo of Taylor with a caption claiming it was a girl named Becky who had died after "snorting marijuana"—a clearly fabricated story. When someone replied, "pretty sure that's Taylor Swift," another user doubled down, replying, "no its becky." The phrase took on a life of its own online, and in perfect Taylor fashion, she joined in on the joke. Not long after, she was spotted walking through New York City wearing a bright yellow shirt that read "no it's becky," and as you'd expect, we lost our shit.

2. Taylor vs. the Heat Lamp

Taylor was once caught on camera glancing around to make sure no one was watching—before touching a heat lamp and immediately burning herself. The intrusive thoughts won. Swifties, of course, turned the clip into a GIF that made the rounds on Tumblr. Taylor took it in stride, later joking, "the day I learned fire is hot." Years later, when a fan teased her for not properly blowing out the firework candles on her birthday cake, she replied: "I don't have like a lot of experience with cake fireworks and god knows when I get close to flames you guys remind me of it later."

3. Yes, Whale!

This one's simple: Taylor was on vacation, filming a video, when she spotted a whale jumping out of the water. Without missing a beat, she shouted, "Yes, whale!"—and of course, we turned it into yet another fan-favorite meme.

4. Wonderfuck

Taylor released a perfume, Wonderstruck, during the *Speak Now* era. Without getting too graphic, a Swiftie once shared on Tumblr that they had worn the scent during a particularly memorable first-time experience in their personal life. Another fan took that story and ran with it—photoshopping a fake ad for the perfume and cheekily renaming it *Wonderfuck*. Later, during a meet and greet, a Swiftie asked Taylor if she was aware of all the wild Tumblr jokes. She confirmed that she was—and specifically mentioned this one. That alone made the whole thing even more hilarious to us.

5. Mother Is Mothering

What started as stan slang quickly became one of the highest forms of praise in the Swiftie fandom. Declaring someone "Mother" is a way of honoring their power, presence, and overall iconic status—and when we say "mother is mothering," we mean she's doing all of the above effortlessly. With Taylor, we often say this when she steps out looking particularly stunning, exuding ultimate confidence and leaving us collectively speechless. It's our way of acknowledging that she's serving everything—the look, the energy, the moment. She doesn't just exist in the spotlight; she commands it.

6. Choose the Right One

Swifties have always felt like a big, supportive family—one built on compassion and kindness. Although that's remained at the heart of it all, like any other close family, we've had our ups and downs. Sometimes fans would compete for Taylor's attention, and jealousy would creep in, especially when we were all young teens. You know, typical sibling energy. But she never hesitated to call us out on our bullshit. One time, during a particularly tense moment in the fandom when certain well-known fans were being rude to each other, she posted a photo of herself wearing gloves labeled "hate" and "love," and told us to "choose the right one." It was her gentle but firm way of saying "I see everything. Behave yourselves." A reminder that while she adored us, she also expected this community to always stay rooted in love. Even back then, she was *mother*.

7. IKYWT (Goat Version)

One of the earliest internet memes came from the *Red* era, when someone replaced the dramatic drop in "I Knew You Were Trouble" with the sound of a screaming goat. And somehow . . . it fit perfectly. The timing and sheer absurdity? Internet gold. The remix immediately went viral, spreading far beyond just the Swiftie fandom. It turned into one of those rare memes that even outsiders somehow knew about. Taylor later said in an interview that she had seen the video and found it hysterical.

8. Rip Me, Died, Dead

During an interview on *The Graham Norton Show*, Taylor listened as Graham read aloud fan reactions to meeting her—many of which described feeling like they were going to die from excitement. Taylor responded with genuine amusement, noting how Swifties always seem to express their love with dramatic, over-the-top phrases involving death. She talked about how she often sees our posts online filled with words like "RIP me," "died," and "dead" in response to anything she does. This was another one of those times where she reminded us that she really does pay attention to the fandom, and that she understands and appreciates just how unhinged we can be.

9. I'm Not Asleep, My Mind Is Alive

Speaking of unhinged, this unforgettable line came from an unintentionally funny moment in Taylor Swift history—and of course, we never let her live it down. After her LASIK eye surgery, Taylor was recovering at home, wearing protective goggles and definitely still a little loopy. Her mom secretly filmed the whole thing, including Taylor getting emotional over a banana and later lying in bed, dramatically saying: "I'm not asleep . . . my mind is alive." When the footage was revealed on *The Tonight Show*, we died. Dead. The delivery, the seriousness, the goggles—it was perfection. Since then, "I'm not asleep, my mind is alive" has become one of our go-to phrases. We say it when we're staying up for surprise songs at 2 a.m. or when *there's a lot going on at the moment*.

10. This Dang Deer

In a 2009 radio interview, Taylor showed off a hidden talent of hers: imitating a Minnesota soccer mom accent. To really sell it, she told a full story in character, with exaggerated Midwest vowels and total drama. The story was about a driving encounter with a deer standing in the middle of the road. The line "This dang deer!" delivered in a thick Minnesota accent instantly became a classic. It's one of those niche references that lives rent-free in our minds, and still resurfaces on the timeline from time to time.

11. The Swift Life App

In 2017, Taylor took her fan engagement to the next level by launching her own social media app, The Swift Life. It was designed as a space where Swifties could connect, share fan art, post messages, and interact—not just with each other but with Taylor too. The app featured exclusive content, emoji-style "Taymojis," and occasional likes or comments from Taylor. Though, like many good things on the internet, it didn't last. Over time, the app became overrun with spam. By early 2019, The Swift Life was officially shut down. Even though it didn't quite stand the test of time, we still remember it very fondly.

12. Tall, Blonde, and Gorgeous Fries Ad

One of the simplest yet most effective Swiftie memes came from—of all places—a McDonald's ad. The ad, meant to describe their golden french fries, read: "Tall, blonde, and gorgeous." But we took one look and thought: That's not fries . . . that's Taylor Swift.

The phrase immediately took off as a running joke in the fandom. We started reposting the ad with captions like "So true bestie" or "McDonald's is a Swiftie confirmed." Even today, whenever Taylor steps out looking radiant, at least one person uses it as a caption.

10. The Fuck Ass Filter

For years, Taylor posted personal photos taken on her Olympus digital camera—these photos often had a strong blue or cool-toned filter that made everything look slightly blurry, dark, and moody, but in a very artsy way. We quickly dubbed it "the fuck ass filter," lovingly roasting the dramatic edit while still eating it up every time she posted a new one. Even though she doesn't post much on social media anymore, her friends will sometimes post photos with the filter, so we automatically know they were taken on Taylor's camera. Anytime new fuck ass filter photos surface online, Swiftie timelines light up with familiar jokes like, "Oh, again with that fucking filter" and "I'd recognize that fuck ass filter anywhere."

CHAPTER FOUR

It's Nice to Have a Friend

While our relationship with Taylor is at the heart of this fandom, the friendships we've formed along the way have equally defined the Swiftie experience. Whether thousands of us are watching livestreams together or going back and forth in the comments section, we are always connected. We even have our own rituals. There's the hand hearts during "Fearless," the double claps in "You Belong With Me," the "1, 2, 3, let's go, bitch!" scream in "Delicate," the dramatic "Take me to church!" moment during the "Don't Blame Me" bridge, the cathartic yell of "You forgive, you forget, but you never let it go!" in "Bad Blood," shouting the city's name during the "Blank Space" bridge, and of course, the "Where are you going, Taylor?" during "Bejeweled." Beyond our fan-made concert traditions, there are the friendship bracelets, the Tumblr posts we've memorized like scripture, the fandom secrets we all instinctively get, and the countless times we've spiraled over a theory that turned out to be absolutely nothing. No one else understands it—and that's what makes it feel sacred. So when people say Swifties are "cultlike," they're not entirely wrong. Most of us do share the same values, speak the same secret language, and rally around the same guiding force. But at the end of the day, we're simply a community of passionate fans who just happen to have impeccable taste in music.

One of the best parts of running @swiftiesforeternity has been getting to talk to fans from all over. Whether it's helping someone secure tickets to a concert, sharing reactions to Taylor news, or receiving the sweetest comments cheering me on in my adventures, this account has introduced me to so many amazing people. Even so, this sense of camaraderie isn't just because I have a platform. It's something we've all experienced. There's a natural kinship that forms in this fandom, and before you know it, you're traveling to concerts together and helping each other snag new merch or concert tickets. Even in a fan base this massive, I've heard from so many fans who are grateful to have found other Swifties online because no one in their everyday life shares their same level of enthusiasm.

Say what you want about social media, but one of its greatest strengths is its ability to bring us together. We've managed to build an entire universe within it. These days, you can find fan accounts for just about anything: celebrities, TV shows, sports teams, and more. It's become a major part of internet culture. But nothing (and yes, I know I'm biased) compares to what we've brought to the table over the last two decades. The fan art, the outfits, the projects, the fundraisers, the dancing, the organized meetups, the *wild joy* . . . we are a fun, artistic, and extremely determined group of individuals. Honestly, I'm even convinced we started the whole social media fan account wave. From the MySpace days to Tumblr, Twitter, Instagram, and TikTok, Swifties have always been ahead of the curve. What I cherish most is that it all started with Taylor. Since 2006, she's been in constant conversation with us, showing up online and always encouraging us. That kind of unity didn't just create a fandom—it created a culture.

The Swiftfluencers

In recent years, the rapidly growing fandom has paved the way for the rise of Swiftie influencers, or what I like to call Swiftfluencers—creators who share their love for Taylor online in unique and creative ways. Many of us, myself included, started out with simple fan pages, but over time we started sharing more of our personal lives, because being a Swiftie is so intricately woven into who we are. While I've been running my account for over a decade, it wasn't until the Eras Tour that my following really took off. But I'm far from the only one. There's Tess (@tessbohne), Kayla (@headfirstfearless), Autumn (@tstourtips), Sarah (@taylorswiftstyled), Andrei (@taylorerastour), Lucas the dog (@iamcalledlucas), Duane (@spartacandleco), Alef (@alefvernonart), Lauren (@laurenlipman)—and so many more. Let's not forget @mermaid.swift, whose unmatched edits are still talked about today. What makes it even more unique is that we've each carved out our own niche. From livestreaming and data tracking to fashion blogging, tour updates, and easter egg commentary, we've all found our own voice and community within the fandom. The most heartwarming part is that millions of both longtime and brand-new Swifties have embraced us. Together, Swiftfluencers have opened the door for so many new fans to join the community and feel right at home. We welcome them in with open arms, show them the ropes, and catch them up on the last two decades of Swiftie lore they've missed.

Whether you're super active in the fandom or just follow along quietly, there's a place for you here. Some fans love to interact and engage daily, while others prefer to observe and enjoy from afar. Really, both are significant. Without each and every one of us, this community wouldn't be what it is today. So if you're one of the quiet ones, just know—you are seen, valued, and appreciated every bit as much as the loud and active Swifties online.

Social media has its drawbacks, but it's also created a space where so much positivity can flourish. Without it, we would never have spent hours watching livestreams together during the Eras Tour. Above all, it's the pillar for so many friendships—and love stories—that have come to life. Nearly every one of us online has made at least one friend, even if it's just through a screen. When

I needed a place to stay while traveling to a show, so many of you messaged offering extra rooms for me and any other Swifties in need. And when a vinyl I posted about wanting sold out, a girl who had been tracking the restocks surprised me by sending one in the mail without me even knowing it. That kind of generosity, from people I've never even met in person, is rare. And yet, for us, it's second nature. Swiftie kindness is real, and it's undoubtedly one of the most uplifting parts of our community.

From Online to In Person

While social media has made it easier than ever to connect with fans online, there's something to be said about being in the same room, face-to-face with fellow Swifties. Sometimes, those times happen spontaneously—like spotting someone out in the wild wearing merch and saying, "I love your shirt!" One fan told me she wears merch every time she goes to the airport, just so other Swifties know they can approach her if they want. Another said she made a new friend in her apartment building simply because she had a Taylor-inspired doormat. Other times, those moments are planned—like the Swiftie cruise out of Miami that sold out instantly, drawing fans of all ages and showing just how far we'd go to spend time with one another.

The cool thing is, the second another Swiftie starts talking to us, any ounce of social anxiety seems to disappear. There's an instant sense of trust, like we already know each other, and in many ways, we do. Whether you exchange a friendship bracelet and make a little small talk or you walk away with a new friend, those interactions are proof that this fandom is one-of-a-kind.

Of course, the most obvious example of in-person Swiftie camaraderie happens at Taylor Swift concerts. When you're in the stadium, you can feel it in your bones. All it takes to start a conversation is walking up to someone and asking, "Do you want to trade friendship bracelets?" It's that easy. Sometimes it even extends beyond the stadium. Fans team up to share flights, hotel rooms, or rides just to make it to a show. For me, it meant traveling to Ohio when I was eighteen to meet a Swiftie I had only ever talked to online and over FaceTime. People around me silently judged, and I couldn't blame them—it did sound a little crazy. But my parents never made me feel that way. They supported my teenage adventures wholeheartedly and encouraged me to build independence, even if it started with a plane ticket and a concert.

That Ohio trip was a milestone for me. It was the first time I had ever traveled alone. I stepped off the plane and was greeted by the girl who had welcomed me into her home for a week. Together we went to one of the *Reputation* Stadium Tour shows, where we finally met so many of the other Swifties we'd known online. Just like on the *1989* World Tour, I was once again surrounded by people who understood this part of me. The girl and I quickly became partners in crime, and that summer, the two of us ended up going to five more shows. What started as a shared love for a single artist turned into a summer full of stories to tell.

We weren't sneaking into clubs or throwing wild parties like typical teens—not that summer, anyway. Our rule-breaking was reserved for much more wholesome adventures: sprinting across the floor mid-show to catch Taylor's performances on the B-stages, and trying every Photoshop trick in the book to get ourselves or our friends onto the floor, even without floor seats. We were rebels in our own right. One night, we met two other girls in our section and instantly clicked. Just two days later, we were back on the road to visit them for a slumber party. That's part of the magic of this fandom—one concert can lead to so much more than just one memory. Fortunately, that was far from the last time I'd have experiences like these.

Nearly a decade later, I found myself in other situations that demonstrated just how easily we're able to go from strangers to friends. The first was at the Super Bowl in February 2025. I'd gone alone and ended up running into a travel influencer who was a big Swiftie and a longtime supporter of my account. He was also sitting by himself, so we decided to walk around the stadium until we found a row of empty seats behind the media section. We sat and watched the game together, cheering for every Chiefs touchdown and every time they showed Taylor on the screen—enough to make up for the buzzkills. Even now, we still keep in touch, treasuring the memories we made that day.

Then on August 13, 2025, when the *New Heights* Taylor episode was airing, I had a flight scheduled, and there was no chance I'd have Wi-Fi to watch and report on it live. So I did what any sane Swiftie would do . . . I changed my flight to an earlier one, even if it meant taking a longer, indirect route. As soon as I got to the Nashville airport, my first flight was delayed, and I started stressing that I might miss my connection. While I was pacing at the gate, two girls came up to me and said they were big Swifties who followed me on Instagram. We started talking and, to our surprise, realized we were all heading to the same final destination; we even had the same connecting flights. I half joked, "Well, if we miss the connection, let's just rent a car and drive." Sure enough, when we landed from our first flight, we sprinted across the terminal only to find the doors had just closed. They wouldn't let us on, and the next flight wasn't until eight that night. We'd still miss the podcast episode, so we had no choice but to rent a *getaway car* and start driving.

We got in and drove over four hours together. First came a full Taylor karaoke session, then conversations where we learned about each other's lives. At one point, I set up my laptop with a hot spot in the back seat so we could all listen to the podcast as I streamed it. By the end of the trip, it didn't feel like bad luck at all. It felt like something we were meant to live. I had been documenting the journey online, and when everyone found out we hadn't made our flight, many commented that they were secretly glad we missed it, because they knew nothing could top a Swiftie road trip with new friends. And honestly, deep down, I had been hoping the same. It was the kind of adventure that could only happen to one of us.

Thanks to this community, I've formed bonds with people I likely wouldn't have crossed paths with otherwise—people who've become part of my real life in the most surreal ways. We've screamed at concerts, cheered during touchdowns, and even found ourselves at award shows together. If there's one thing I've learned, it's that friendships can begin in the most unexpected places, and you never know who will become a part of your story, even if just for an era.

It's a Love Story

I've witnessed some pretty incredible things the last decade or so, but one tale in particular has always stuck with me. A longtime

Swiftie who often commented on my posts once messaged me out of the blue. Not to talk about Taylor, but to thank me for running my account. He told me he'd connected with someone in the comments section, and after a few replies back and forth, they moved to DMs. Eventually, they planned a trip to meet in person and fell in love. He described it as finding his missing piece—further serving as proof that hopeless romantics and Swifties go hand in hand. He mentioned how many little coincidences, or *invisible strings*, had subtly tied them together all along. What struck me the most wasn't just their story—it was how many lives this fandom has touched, all because of Taylor. Her music brought two strangers together in a comments section, but it's brought together so many more of us than we could ever imagine. From "Love Story" proposals during concerts to awkwardly timed engagements in front of Taylor (you know the one), it's clear that this fandom has never been just about the music; it's always been about us finding each other through it.

There's an unspoken understanding that, even if we've never met, we'd show up for one another if needed. The friendship bracelet revolution may have been sparked by "You're On Your Own, Kid," but friendships between Swifties began long before. It began in 2006, when one girl with a guitar unknowingly gave millions of people a reason to unite. Since then, we've carried what she started and built something of our own—a universe where passion, expression, and belonging thrive. And that? We wouldn't trade it for anything.

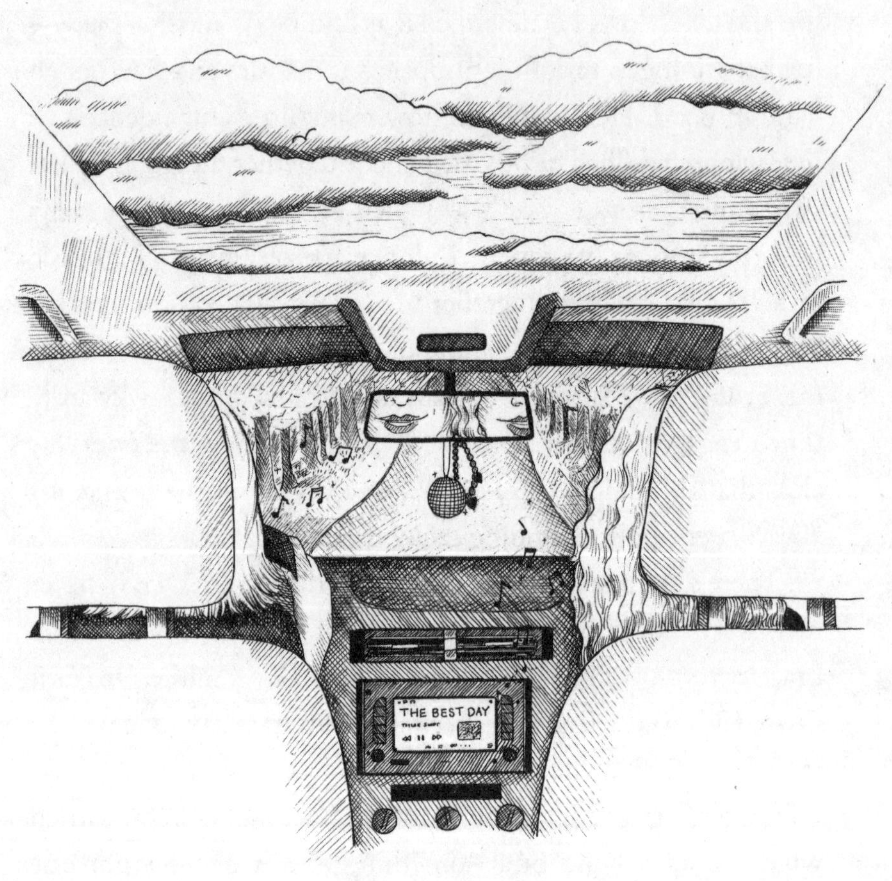
THE BEST DAY

CHAPTER FIVE

The Best Day

A friend once told me that before anyone knew who Taylor was, their dad had been on a work trip with Scott Swift. Even then Scott was already raving about his daughter's talent. He was so certain she'd make it as a musician that he gave my friend's dad a guitar pick with Taylor's name on it, declaring she would be a famous singer one day. My friend's dad laughed it off at the time, assuming it was just another proud parent's dream. Little did he know he was holding a piece of history in his hand, given to him by the most legendary guitar-pick-giver of all time, a gesture that proved Scott always knew that his daughter was destined for greatness.

From early on in Taylor's career, her parents, Andrea and Scott, along with her brother, Austin, have played meaningful roles—so much so that Taylor refers to themselves as a family business. For us, they've always felt like part of the package. Andrea has long been known for chatting with fans at shows, offering heartfelt thank-yous for supporting her daughter's dream. Scott, of course, became famous for passionately handing out his custom guitar picks, and Austin has consistently shown up with unwavering support, both in the crowd and behind the scenes, handling the television licensing of her music.

When I had the chance to spend time with them myself, what struck me most was how genuinely welcoming they were. Austin was fully engaged, asking questions and making us feel like part of their inner circle. Scott was the proud dad, effortlessly gaining our attention with behind-the-scenes stories about what it's like to be Taylor Swift's father. I totally understand now why Taylor describes him as a "social savant"—he loves to talk and make everyone feel like his new best friend. And Andrea moved through the room, hugging everyone like the fandom's honorary mom—because, well, she really is. Despite Taylor's extraordinary level of fame, there was something refreshingly real and down-to-earth about them, a family that made you feel instantly at home.

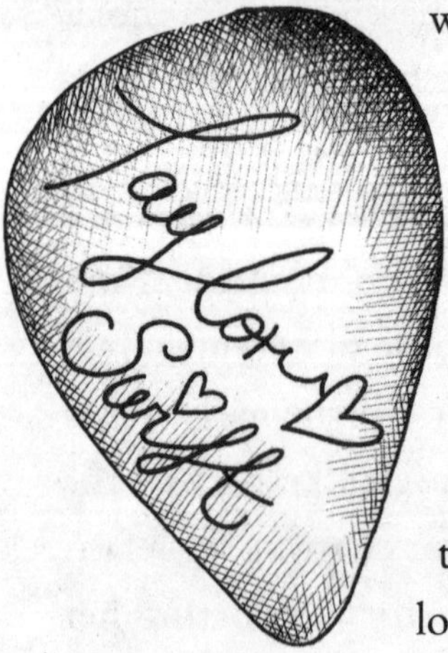

Their involvement has extended far beyond what we see. As we now know, when it came time to fight for Taylor's music, it was Andrea and Austin who flew to Los Angeles to negotiate on her behalf, making clear just how much it would mean to her to buy back her masters. There's something profoundly moving about the fact that the same people who once packed up their lives and moved to Nashville so Taylor could write and create her music were also the ones who helped her get it back. It was Andrea who ultimately called Taylor with the news that she had reclaimed her entire life's work, a full-circle moment in a long journey that began when she was just fifteen years old.

During one of the final Eras Tour shows, Taylor performed a mash-up of "Never Grow Up" and "The Best Day." Though "The Best Day" was written for her mom, it's also a snapshot from her childhood with her dad and brother. Blended with "Never Grow Up," a song about innocence that's rooted in nostalgia, the performance became an emotional tribute to all of them. In the VIP tent, Andrea teared up as Scott embraced her from behind, soon joined by Austin wrapping his arms around both of them. In that moment, it was apparent: They're still in awe of Taylor, and appreciative of each other. They were the original Swifties. The very first members of our community. Fittingly, Taylor's music has gone on to help so many of us strengthen bonds within our own families, a legacy only one like theirs could inspire.

Mothers and Daughters

At one of the Miami Eras Tour shows, I found myself sitting behind a young mother and her daughter. At one point, the mom turned to me and said, "I just want you to know I follow you on Instagram, and you're the reason I became such a big Swiftie. Now I'm here at the show with my daughter." Exchanges like that mean everything to me, but even more, they reflect the beautiful ripple effect Taylor has had on all of our lives.

"The Best Day" is my mom's favorite song. She's always loved how close Taylor is with her own mom, and I feel incredibly lucky to share that kind of bond with mine. Whenever my friends bailed on me in high school, my mom would "pull an Andrea Swift" and take me to the mall. When I first became enthralled by Taylor's music, she sat through every single YouTube video and song I showed her, seeming to enjoy it just as much as I did. By listening to the lyrics I resonated with, she was able to better understand the feelings I was trying to process as a teenager. After hours upon hours spent screaming songs in the car and dozens of concerts attended together, we somehow became our own version of Lorelai and Rory Gilmore. I know we have Taylor, in large part, to thank for that.

My story is just one example—there are countless mother-daughter Swiftie duos who've connected through Taylor's music over the years. For many of us, it's become a tradition to see the shows together. These days, getting concert tickets isn't exactly easy (don't worry, we'll get to that), but moms and daughters still manage to make up a big portion of the crowd. Whether it's a quick road trip or a long flight across the ocean, traveling to see Taylor has become part of the experience, creating soul-deep memories that last a lifetime. But there are also the smaller, more budget-friendly joys—the late-night album release parties, the excitement of dissecting every new lyric, and the race to get to Target early on release days to buy physical copies and limited-edition vinyls. Taylor herself used to join in on the tradition, appearing at her local Target to buy the album and surprise fans who were doing the same. And we must not forget the everyday car rides, with Taylor's songs playing on a loop. No special occasion needed. For so many, her music has become a bridge between generations, bonding us even when nothing else can.

Since Taylor has been around for two decades, many of us who grew up alongside her are now adults with children of our own, kids who probably first heard *Fearless* while still in the womb. An entire generation has been born into the fandom by default, and now those same kids are dancing and singing beside their moms at the tours. It's incredible to see how she's impacted the lives of multiple generations. The songs that once got us through our youth are now the ones helping our children through theirs. Even the littlest Swifties, often called "Taylor Tots" online, get to experience the camaraderie in their own ways—they throw Taylor-themed birthday celebrations, dress up as her for Halloween, make and trade friendship bracelets, and twirl around the living room learning performance choreography. If they're lucky enough to be at a show, you'll find them in matching outfits with their moms, wide-eyed and radiant.

Fathers and Daughters

It's not just mothers and daughters who bond over Taylor Swift. It's fathers and daughters too. Her influence extends past girlhood nostalgia or teenage anthems; it weaves its way into households, turning everyone, whether they intended to be or not, into a Swiftie.

One viral reel captured it perfectly. Author and influencer Carlos Whittaker shared a side-by-side video of himself driving his two young daughters to the *Fearless* Tour back in 2010, and then again to the Eras Tour in 2023. Only this time, the girls are grown, and Carlos is behind the wheel in nearly the same outfit. The full-circle moment had everyone emotional, including Taylor herself, who commented on the post: "MY HEART WAS NOT PREPARED," followed by many, many emojis. Whether they've been fans from the beginning or joined in because their kids dragged them along, dads have become a crucial part of our fandom story. They're the ones holding extra friendship bracelets, belting out lyrics, and wearing their "Swiftie Dad" shirts like badges of honor. And now, thanks to Taylor's unexpected association with the NFL, Swifties are returning the favor. We're tuning in to football games, learning the rules, and getting just as hyped over touchdown passes as we do during the bridge of "Cruel Summer." You're welcome, Dads.

Everyone remembers where they were on Sunday, September 24, 2023. It's a date engraved into the Swiftie history books, or at least this one. I remember every detail. I had just finished loading my car with an unreasonable amount of pumpkin-flavored Trader Joe's snacks when I sat down in the driver's seat to do my usual pre-drive scroll—you know, my "are there any Taylor updates" routine. Then I saw them. Photos of Taylor in a box at a Kansas City Chiefs game . . . with Travis Kelce's mom, Donna Kelce. I was floored. Taylor and Travis?! Everyone on planet Earth had tried to shoot their shot with Taylor, so the fact that his public, "metal as hell" callout on his podcast actually worked was shocking, and also kind of epic. I'm sure he was just as surprised as we were. That day, it became official: Taylor had entered Chiefs Kingdom and, by extension, so did we. If you had told me a few years ago that I'd soon be watching grown men throw balls on my TV every Sunday, I would've cackled in your face. I had no idea I had signed up for this when I became a Swiftie. Yet, here we were, suddenly invested in touchdowns, tight ends, and the number 87. We were now all football fans. Kansas City Chiefs fans. TNT fans. Some of us had a lot of stats to catch up on.

This was the moment dads everywhere stepped up to the plate. It was finally their time to shine! I can only imagine how big my dad smiled when I called him and asked, "Are you watching the Chiefs game?" He's always loved football, but neither my brothers nor I were into it as kids, so he eventually stopped watching religiously. Instead, he chose to spend his limited time away from work doing things we cared about. Now, a decade later, the tables had turned in his favor. I was the one asking him to turn on the game so we could watch it together over FaceTime and he could explain the rules to me. Needless to say, he was thrilled. The next time I visited home, we watched a game side by side, something we had never done before. At last we had something in common that we were both equally excited about—even if for wildly different reasons. Soon thereafter, I started getting texts from other men in my life during every single Chiefs game: "You watching?" My uncle—who I rarely text—and I essentially started a weekly football thread. I couldn't believe it. Somehow, I had gone from watching only the yearly Super Bowl to becoming the designated football commentator in my family group chat. "Football expert" might be a stretch, but I'd gladly add it right under "Swiftie for eternity" on my résumé. And the craziest part? A lot of us actually started to appreciate the game, tuning in even when Taylor wasn't there.

Dads all over the country grew closer to their daughters, while uncles bonded with their nieces, grandfathers with their granddaughters, and partners with each other—boyfriends, girlfriends, husbands, and wives alike. But it was a two-way street. While we leaned in to their favorite sport, they started opening their minds to our favorite artist. Maybe they just wanted to understand how one woman managed to strengthen their relationships simply by attending football games. Regardless, we were eager to tell them all about her.

The Cetaphil commercial during the 2024 Super Bowl brought our stories to life, uniting two seemingly different fandoms—Swifties and football fans—and showing how a shared passion can dissolve the barriers that often divide us. The ad told a simple tale: A dad asks his daughter to watch the game, but she's uninterested. That is, until the announcer on TV says, "And there she is . . . the most famous fan of the game." Her curiosity is piqued. Later, her dad walks into her room wearing a friendship bracelet and hands her a jersey with the number 13, while he wears one with 89, a nod to Taylor's *1989* album. She smiles, puts it on, and joins him on the couch. Together, they watch the game, grinning. They didn't need to say much. We all understood the meaning. Family members who had never truly connected before suddenly found something to share. We learned *how to ball*—figuratively and literally (yes, many of us finally mastered the art of throwing a football). And dads, in return, got a crash course on one of the greatest philosophers and writers in history. Sorry, did you think I meant Aristotle? Obviously, it's Taylor Swift.

A Family Affair

Being a Swiftie has become part of our family's identity. Taylor's music plays on the car ride to school, during family road trips, while cleaning the house, or anytime there's a speaker nearby. It's present in our everyday lives. Parents and significant others walk through the door after work with a smile, casually asking, "Any Taylor news today?"—not because they're keeping up, but because they know that you are. Tour films run in the background like comfort TV shows. Holidays are filled with Taylor-themed gifts: vinyl records, merch, bracelets, books, and the many collector's edition magazines you always pause in the checkout line to flip through and try not to buy. Christmas trees are decorated with Swiftie ornaments. Let's be honest—album release nights feel more magical than actual holidays, becoming a heartwarming family tradition.

Then there are the humorous moments that become part of the family lore: explaining what a "vault track" is to a grandparent who thinks it has something to do with banking, watching a dad try to understand what makes an outfit *Red*-coded versus *1989*-coded, or teaching everyone the vocabulary—what an era is, how track fives are usually the most heartbreaking, why snakes are so important—which has become its own Swiftie rite of passage.

Family trips have been planned entirely around concerts. Especially during the Eras Tour, when it was somehow cheaper to hop on a plane to Europe than to get a ticket in your own city. Leave it to Swifties to turn that chaos into adventure. I know moms who turned the frustrating ticket search into multigenerational girls' trips with their daughters and their own moms. I've gotten messages from men who surprised their kids, their wives, even their own parents with tickets to a show. Those who tagged along "just to be supportive" left the show as fans themselves. We've all seen it happen—men who thought they were too masculine or too cool to like Taylor, ending the night by posting, "Okay . . . I get it now." Just ask former NFL player J. J. Watt.

One night, I sat near a woman—likely in her seventies or eighties—who had come to the Eras Tour by herself. She was reserved, but you could see the awe on her face as she watched the stage. When nearby fans offered her friendship bracelets, her whole face lit up. It was a striking reminder of the kind of space we've created. No matter your age, gender, or reason for being there, once you step inside that stadium, you're embraced by something far greater than any one person.

Taylor's music has marked some of the biggest moments of our lives. For some, that's walking down the aisle to "Lover" or "You Are In Love." Others have chosen "Enchanted" for their first dance or wiped away tears while dancing to "The Best Day" with their moms. From birthdays to baby showers, graduations to memorials, there always seems to be a lyric that fits perfectly.

Thousands of people have reached out to tell me how their relationships with family members have improved because of Taylor. My own brother used to tease me endlessly for being so obsessed with her when I was a kid. Until one day, he finally saw the light. Now, years later, he's a dedicated Swiftie, wanting to travel to multiple shows, and is the first one to text whenever she breaks yet another record. For that, I have his longtime partner Patrick to thank, since he helped me bring him over to the "good side." Through our love of Taylor, the three of us have grown close, and we now even have a group chat that absolutely explodes anytime something happens. What once felt like a one-sided interest has become a full-blown family affair.

Being a Swiftie doesn't just live in your shower singalongs or your morning scroll through fan account updates—it seeps into the rhythm of everyday family life. It shows up in the way your mom randomly starts singing a Taylor song at dinner, or how your dad casually drops a lyric into conversation to make you laugh. It's in the group chats lighting up with new theories, or in your sibling saying they're grateful for existing at the same time as Taylor Swift. At some point, what started as one person's fandom turned into a treasured custom. In a time when it's way too easy to feel disconnected, Taylor has given us a reason to grow closer to our parents, our siblings, our grandparents, our partners, and our chosen families.

CHAPTER SIX

The Swiftie Effect

Swifties have become one of the most influential communities. At times, it feels like there's nothing we can't do. What we've built is powerful, authentic, and enduring. Whether we're uplifting small businesses, flooding hospitals and charities with donations, or just making someone's day with a friendship bracelet and a compliment, our reach extends far beyond anything we can tangibly see. Alongside Taylor, we've created an everlasting impact.

The Swiftie effect began long ago—our first lasting imprint being on Taylor herself, as we rallied behind her to leave a *permanent mark* on country music. Then again when we supported her in taking over the pop genre. Of course, Taylor got to where she is because of her talent and relentless dedication to her craft. Still, through it all, she never walked that path alone, because we were always beside her, supporting her every step of the way. If she pivoted to rap music tomorrow, we'd still have her charting at number one within seconds. Remember in 2014, when eight seconds of white noise was accidentally released? It topped the iTunes charts simply because it had her name attached. That's the level of belief we have in her. We show up in every way we can, making the brands she wears and even the sports she watches part of our own lives too.

Over the years, brands have taken notice of our ability to make a difference, and honestly, how could they not? After everything we've influenced, it was impossible to ignore. They saw us as more than just a fan base; we were a global market. With over $2 billion grossed from the Eras Tour alone and massive economic booms in every city Taylor performed in (or that we traveled to), we practically created our own economy around her.

Style

We've always had a major influence on the brands Taylor partners with. I know I'm not the only one who still has a few pairs from the Taylor x Keds collection tucked away. Capital One, Target, Diet Coke, and CoverGirl are just a few of the other companies that have felt the full force of the Swiftie effect. When I was young, I wanted it all. It only escalated once I became an adult with my own wallet. First it was makeup and perfume, and more recently, a lavender tennis skort she made go viral. We do more than just shop. We spark trends, drive demand, and turn everyday items into cultural phenomena.

During the *1989* era, I went back-to-school shopping with my mom and wanted nothing but high-waisted shorts, skirts, and matching crop tops. She knew exactly why and, being the supportive parent she is, let me pick out several Taylor-inspired outfits. Walking through the hallways in them didn't just feel like getting dressed for school; it felt like stepping into my own *1989* era at fifteen, those formative years when I was figuring out who I was and what I liked. Tumblr was filled with Swifties re-creating her looks: red lips, cat-eye liner, vintage sunglasses, and high-waisted sets. It was like we all silently agreed to embrace the aesthetic together. Taylor herself would leave sweet comments and likes on our posts. Who needed anyone else's approval when we had hers? Very parasocial, I know.

With the rise of fashion blogs and style accounts, we could identify Taylor's entire look—down to the shoes and jewelry—within minutes of her stepping outside. We didn't just admire the outfits, we bought them immediately. Or we tried to. Even now, in our twenties, thirties, forties, and beyond, Taylor is still our style icon. Thankfully, many of us are at the stage where we can finally afford some of the pieces she wears—well, at least the ones not custom-made by designers or those with a price tag that screams "*You do* not *belong with me*."

One single lyric in "You're On Your Own, Kid" telling us to "make the friendship bracelets" ignited a viral trend. While the song came from *Midnights*, the craze exploded during the Eras Tour. What was once a niche craft became a booming industry, thanks to us who took Taylor's words literally and turned it into our mission. Suddenly, friendship bracelets weren't just accessories, they were currency. If you showed up to a show without any? Don't worry. You would still walk out with an armful. But the friendship bracelets were only the start of what was to come. The tour also kicked off a costume revolution. Every brand began selling Eras Tour–inspired outfits, and new shops popped up just to keep up with the demand. Sequins, sparkles, fringed jackets, glitter boots—anything that looked remotely like something Taylor might wear onstage flew off the shelves. At this point, businesses know: If it's Swiftie-approved, it's essentially a gold mine.

Your Vinyl Shelf

It was November 29, 2024, at 5 a.m. My mom was FaceTiming me from downstairs. "Are you awake? We have to leave in a few minutes if you want to get *The Tortured Poets Department: The Anthology* vinyl," she said. "Yes! I'm throwing on a hoodie! Meet you in the garage!" I replied. At this point, it seemed easier to become president than to get your hands on one of the limited edition vinyls. I still hadn't recovered from missing out on the heart-shaped *Lover: Live from Paris* edition. However, I had hope this time. I was home for the holidays, which meant I was back out in the country, where I figured my chances were better than in a big city. We pulled into the first Target at exactly 5:05 a.m. and bolted through the parking lot. Just as I caught sight of the vinyl display, I saw another girl grab the last copy. It happened in slow motion, like one of those tragic scenes in a movie. It was the kind of heartbreak you can't even prepare for. Still, I grabbed a couple of Eras Tour books—small wins—but no vinyls. My mom, who's always been ride-or-die, decided we were making a morning of it. We went on a full Target tour of Connecticut.

This was no longer a mission. It was a quest. At the second store, they had vinyls, but the cashiers were keeping them behind the registers and limiting them to two per person. Unfortunately, they were already gone by the time I got in line. Then came the third Target. It was one of those forgotten stores that barely ever stocks vinyls. This was Taylor Swift, though, and clearly someone at corporate understood the assignment. There they were: untouched, glorious, and waiting for us. My mom and I each grabbed one, plus an extra for a giveaway I had planned for my Instagram followers. We drove home triumphant with smiles on our faces. It was still dark outside when we walked through the front door at 6:30 a.m., arms full of bags and still bundled in our furry jackets. My dad took one look at us and shook his head like we were absolutely out of our minds.

I documented our entire Target journey online, and as I scrolled through my feed, I saw Swifties everywhere doing the exact same thing. Some had been camped outside stores since 2 a.m. in the freezing cold. None of it surprised me. This is just how we operate. At the time, we didn't know how limited the *Anthology* vinyl would be, so we treated it like *The Hunger Games*. Fans began posting photos of themselves clutching their vinyls like trophies. Others offered up their extra copies to those online who couldn't grab one. What looked like madness in the aisles of stores was really a glimpse into the impact we've had on how music is consumed today.

At a time when many artists had nearly stopped pressing vinyl, we helped fuel its revival. When Taylor decided vinyl was back in style and began releasing collectible variants, we showed up. Some of us bought them all, others just one to display on the wall, even if we didn't own a record player. *The Life of a Showgirl* went on to break the all-time US record for the largest vinyl sales week in history, with over 1.334 million copies sold. It was proof that when Swifties decide something matters, the industry takes note, and eventually everyone else starts prioritizing it too. We'd seen it before, back in 2014, when the *1989* album cover kicked off the resurgence of Polaroid photos. From instant film to spinning records, we don't just follow culture. We create it.

Journey to Swiftiehood

I've lost count of how many times I've heard someone say, "I'm a fan. I listen to her music, but I don't know if I'd call myself a Swiftie." That hesitation comes from the weight the word "Swiftie" carries—it signals a deeper kind of dedication, and everybody knows it. Yet as Taylor herself has said, you don't need to spend hours decoding easter eggs to belong. It's more than okay to simply enjoy the music. However, we still carry an unspoken responsibility: turning as many haters and casual fans into Swifties as we can throughout our lifetime. Maybe they're skeptics. Maybe they've just never taken the time to really listen to all of her music. Whatever the reason, we see it as both a challenge and an opportunity.

In college, my freshman-year roommate Casey definitely wasn't a Swiftie. She wasn't a hater, per se, but she admitted that the media's portrayal of Taylor had left her with a negative impression. I couldn't really blame her. The media hadn't been kind to Taylor at all back then. In fact, it rarely ever is, so if you don't look further, you could mistake their headlines as reality. But if you know anything about me—or about Swifties in general—then you know that wouldn't last long. I felt a personal duty to change Casey's mind. Slowly but surely, I introduced her to the music, the lyrics, and the lore. Before long, she wasn't just a fan of Taylor; she was invested, trying to turn others into Swifties too.

On August 21, 2019, I brought her with me to New York City for the *Good Morning America* performance Taylor was doing live in Central Park the next morning. We checked in to our hotel, dropped our bags, and made our way to the venue. It was a free show, which meant the line already spanned several blocks. We got in line at 10 p.m. and spent the next nine hours bonding with other fans under the city lights. Thoughtfully, Taylor sent her team to drop off pizzas for those of us waiting overnight. We sang, chatted, and did our best to stay awake. By 7 a.m., we were half-asleep and barely functioning, but it was finally our turn to move forward. I won't lie: Seeing Taylor after staying up for twenty-four hours straight was a little surreal. The memory is a blur—very different from the other times I had seen her live. I remember singing "ME!" with the rest of the crowd, then crashing in a cab back to the hotel, the driver having to wake us up when we arrived. We slept the rest of the day but woke up just in time for the *Lover* album release that night. Since then, Casey's Spotify Wrapped has included Taylor Swift every single year. There's nothing quite like introducing someone to the magic for the first time. We've all done it. Whether it's a roommate, a family member, a partner, or a friend. When they finally get it? When they hear that lyric or experience that show? That's when you know you've changed their life for the better.

Chiefs and Swifties: From Friendship Bracelets to Football

Shout-out to all of you who were already proud members of both Chiefs Kingdom and Swiftie Nation before the TNT effect ever took place, and an even bigger shout-out to the couple who somehow predicted the future by dressing up as Travis and Taylor for Halloween years before they'd even met. The Instagram post by @_makaylastephens_ read, "I don't know any world in which Taylor Swift + Travis Kelce would be in the same room together, but apparently in this one they're married?" And yes, I'm still not over it.

There's no denying the Swiftie effect on football since Taylor showed up at that first Chiefs game. Travis Kelce's jersey sales skyrocketed and game viewership surged, especially among women, who suddenly made up half of the NFL's audience. Even fans in places where "football" meant something else entirely began tuning in, just to be part of it all. Perhaps most importantly, that was the day we welcomed in a brand-new wave of Swifties. Just as we loved Travis because Taylor did, his fans began loving Taylor because he did. I'm not sure who had more to learn: us with touchdowns and penalties, or them with two decades of Swiftie history to catch up on. Either way, both sides did their research, and now we are more well-rounded humans who appreciate all of it—the artist, the player, and the game.

Thanks to livestreaming, most of our 2023 and 2024 weekends were already booked up with Eras Tour shows. Soon enough, scheduling conflicts began popping up as Chiefs games and Eras Tour performances were happening at the same time. More than once, I found myself watching a game on TV, streaming a concert on my phone, and posting real-time updates on Instagram like it was my full-time job. And well, it kind of was. This unexpected crossover united two of the most passionate fan bases and turned them into one major powerhouse. Together, we've influenced businesses, boosted economies, and created a cultural shift far bigger than anything a single artist—or tight end—could have ever foreseen.

Once Chiefs games entered our fandom, Kansas City businesses began to feel the ripple effect too. Luckily, Chiefs fans already understood what true dedication looked like, so when Swifties joined in, the result was explosive. Taylor's game-day outfits became a highlight for us. She often wore local Kansas City vintage pieces paired with jewelry or hats from small businesses. While some joked that she put Travis Kelce "on the map," what she really did was put dozens of small, often women-run businesses on the map instead.

The second she walked down the stadium tunnel, we all became fashion detectives, trying to identify the origin of every piece she wore. Quickly, brands went viral on social media, gaining tens of thousands of new followers, and whatever she had on instantly sold out. Remember the glitter freckles she wore at the

October 7, 2024, game? Per Bloomberg, the small brand, Fazit, saw a 3,500 percent spike in sales immediately after. Two weeks later, glitter freckles were everywhere! Stocked at Urban Outfitters, featured in beauty tutorials, and glistening on every face at the Eras Tour stop in Miami.

Taylor had also worn a little jersey ring from a local Kansas City shop called EB and Co.—a dainty piece with the number 87 on it—to a Chiefs game back in January 2024. That one moment changed everything for the local business. Orders started flooding in. Eight months later, when I spoke with the store's founder, she told me she had *finally* caught up on ring orders. Because of us, she was able to put a down payment on her dream home. It only reaffirmed what we've always known: Anything Taylor touches—amplified by Swifties everywhere—takes on a life of its own.

In September 2024, I found myself headed to Kansas City to cohost an event with EB and Co. I'll admit, I was hesitant at first. I kept thinking, *What if no one shows up?* The imposter syndrome was very real. I'm not a celebrity. I don't even like calling myself an influencer. I usually say "fanfluencer," because at the end of the day, I'm just a fan who happened to turn her love for an artist into something more. But the store believed in the Swiftie effect. And they were right. Moms came with their mini Swifties. Girlfriends brought their boyfriends. Groups of best friends showed up, all wearing Eras-inspired outfits and stacks of friendship bracelets. The energy in that room was indescribable—full of nonstop chatter about favorite albums, upcoming shows, and predictions. It was the kind of warmth that makes you feel like you've known these strangers your whole life. If there's ever a room full of us, you can bet it'll be the safest, most welcoming space you'll ever walk into.

Just when we thought the football crossover couldn't get any bigger, it did. In the summer of 2025, I attended the Tight End University concert in Nashville, an event hosted by NFL tight ends, including none other than Travis Kelce. I was front row, excited for the country artist lineup, when I noticed Taylor upstairs in the VIP section. I had a suspicion she might do an impromptu performance, but I didn't let myself fully believe it—until I saw it with my own eyes as she walked out to close the show with Kane Brown.

The second the opening notes of "Shake It Off" rang out in that tiny venue of about six hundred people, the whole place burst into cheers. Football fans, country fans, and Swifties suddenly became one voice, shouting the lyrics together like we'd been part of the same fan base all along. It was yet another reminder of how seamlessly Taylor bridges worlds that rarely collide. What made it even more indelible was how spontaneous it was. Taylor had scribbled the chords down on a piece of paper for the band, borrowed Chase Rice's guitar, and decided minutes before to just go for it, confident the crowd would go wild. It felt so intimate. We hadn't seen her perform in a venue that size since the early days of her career, and for a few minutes, it felt like we'd been transported back in time.

Never Be So Clever You Forget to Be Kind

The day in 2024 after Taylor visited patients at Children's Mercy Hospital in Kansas City was her thirty-fifth birthday. I remember seeing Swifties across social media suggest we each donate $13 to our local hospitals in her honor. It was such a small gesture that no doubt made a meaningful difference when carried out by thousands of us. I wish we could pull the numbers!

That day at the hospital, Taylor asked a little girl named Tinley Raaf what she wanted for Christmas. Tinley said a Dyson Airwrap. The very next day, on Taylor's birthday, that exact gift showed up in Tinley's hospital room with a note that read:

T— In case Santa doesn't come through . . . Love, Taylor

After I spoke to Tinley's mom on Instagram, she kindly gave me permission to share the story and the video. The post reached millions of people on every social media platform. I then asked if I could include a donation link to help with Tinley's medical bills. Shortly after my posting it, Swifties raised over $6,000. It was one of those acts that reminded me of the goodness still very much alive around us, and how our fandom is such a beautiful piece of it. Then it happened again.

In June 2025, Taylor visited Joe DiMaggio Children's Hospital in Florida, signing Eras Tour books for patients and spending time with families. One of those families was facing overwhelming medical expenses and decided to sell their signed Eras Tour book online for $500. They didn't want to, but they needed the money. One fan bought the book and told the family to keep it, then did what Swifties do best and shared the family's GoFundMe link across social media. Within hours, we rallied behind the cause, and by the next day the fundraiser had surpassed $51,000. Many of those donations, once again, were made in increments of $13. It was our nod to Taylor, and it didn't stop there. We helped raise money for several other families at the hospital Taylor had visited that day.

Then there was a Swiftie named Lily Tomlinson. In early 2025, we learned about a thirteen-year-old from Pennsylvania who had been diagnosed with an aggressive brain tumor. Her mom reached out to a small Swiftie crafting group asking for blankets and hats to bring Lily comfort during radiation. What followed was nothing short of amazing. Signed CDs, handwritten letters, and thousands of friendship bracelets began arriving at her home from all over the world. The family's GoFundMe link spread across social media, and within weeks we had raised over $83,000. The hashtag #SwiftiesForLily trended, bringing light into the family's darkest season. Lily said that the outpouring of support helped her realize she wasn't alone—that there were people out there who cared about her. She tragically passed away on July 25, 2025, but her final months were filled with reminders of just how loved she was and forever will be.

Seemingly Iconic

We've already seen how far our reach goes, spreading across fashion, sports, small businesses, and into people's lives. But do you remember the time we caught the attention of a condiment brand? The sensation was born when a photo surfaced of Taylor with a plate holding one chicken nugget, ketchup, and what a fan described as "seemingly ranch." That single post prompted another viral moment in the fandom, adding to our long list of inside jokes. Only this time, people outside the fandom joined in too. Within days, Heinz announced a limited-edition Ketchup and Seemingly Ranch sauce, and to top it off, the Empire State Building lit up red and white in honor of the tweet. Just for us. It wasn't long before every brand was posting their own versions, and fans were even dressing up as "seemingly ranch" for the Eras Tour. I'm still not entirely sure how or why it took off the way it did, but it's one of those absurdly specific moments we'll always remember, once again proving that when it comes to Swifties, no industry is off-limits.

Taking on the Streaming Industry

Now that we've discussed leaving our mark on an industry I never thought we'd touch, let's go back to a time when we helped Taylor alter the music industry itself. Specifically, the realm of streaming. In 2014, Taylor made streaming platforms tremble when she pulled her entire catalog from Spotify as part of her stand for fair artist compensation. Then, in 2015, she wrote an open letter to Apple Music, publicly calling them out for not paying artists during users' free three-month trials. Less than twenty-four hours later, Apple responded to her letter and announced they were reversing the policy immediately. That move didn't just make headlines. It made history.

In 2017, Taylor put her catalog back on Spotify, both as a thank-you to us and in recognition of the platform's improvements in financially supporting artists. Not only did this mark the beginning of Taylor's fight for artist rights, but it also showed everyone how much space and control we hold in the industry.

Apple and Spotify, two of the biggest companies on the planet, were willing to bend over backward for her because they knew her army of Swifties would migrate from their platform if they didn't.

Tayimpact

When Taylor Swift announces an album, every single person stops what they're doing to listen. Within hours, the colors of her new era become everyone's new favorite color. Skyscrapers, sports leagues, restaurants, cruise lines, beauty brands, and even government accounts pivot to join in, posting content they know we'll appreciate. Landmark buildings glow in that color. Olive Garden dresses a breadstick in sequins of that color. Airlines post their planes against skies of that color. Marketing teams scrap entire campaigns just to keep up. News outlets cover album releases live like breaking news, and Swiftfluencers like myself are suddenly treated like cultural experts, brought on to live national TV to decode easter eggs and explain to the masses what it all means.

Some of us call out of work or skip school on release day just to soak in the new music and celebrate. Even if we don't, we know that in our offices and classrooms it will be the only thing most people talk about for weeks. At this point, if you're not a Swiftie, you're the minority. Taylor wields a rare kind of influence; one money can't buy and imitation can't replicate. It's not marketing. It's decades of trust, loyalty, and legacy built between us. It's why an album announcement becomes a worldwide sensation. She isn't just a singer. She's a once-in-a-generation force in human form, who can turn an ordinary day into a headline and make the entire world pause to watch.

Taylor's influence has always transcended music, but together we've created something unprecedented—a domino effect that has reached economies, redefined culture, and changed millions of lives. The reason we've been able to move mountains comes down to one simple truth. As social media rose and life became a blur of fleeting fads and shallow connections, Taylor chose depth and intention. She let us truly know her and gave us something constant and real—people to anchor us, songs to carry with us. So when people wonder why we're such an influential community, the answer is simple: It's because of her.

What we should all also recognize is that we are a legacy within a legacy. Taylor may have started the story, but together we've turned it into a series. Whether it's buying something she wears, raising money for charity, setting trends, or standing with her in every fight for justice, we've already left our mark. Dare I say, *That's a real fucking legacy to leave*.

these memories break

CHAPTER SEVEN

THE TOURS

Each Taylor Swift tour has its own distinct personality, and choosing a favorite one is as impossible as picking a favorite song. Every tour marks a new chapter in both her life and ours, and with each one, new traditions are born. There's something so unifying about finally gathering in person with your people, the same fans you've bonded with online for years, to experience something you've all been looking forward to. While her albums define an era, it's the tours that bring them to life in the most spectacular way. From Taylor dramatically tossing a chair off a platform during the *Fearless* Tour to the fireworks erupting at the perfect time during "Dear John" on the *Speak Now* World Tour to the chilling mash-up of "Enchanted" and "Wildest Dreams" on the *1989* World Tour, each one holds a special place in our hearts. Even the performances we've watched through shaky fan videos, pixelated livestreams, and tour films have somehow made us feel as if we were right there in the crowd.

Taylor has always said that performing live is one of her favorite parts of what she does. You can feel the passion she holds, the energy she brings, and the perfectionism she strives for and reaches, night after night. These shows are fully realized emotional experiences that live in our bodies and minds for years. Some would even say we go through withdrawal afterward. Sometimes, we even get amnesia. Whether it's your first time seeing her live or your thirteenth, there's an electricity that fills the air the second she steps onstage.

For us, being a Swiftie has never been passive. It's an exhilarating, never-ending adventure that we all get to take part in. When it comes to the tours, we show up, we scream, we laugh, and we cry. Then we want to do it all over again the very next day. Because these tours are so much more than a well-planned performance. They aren't defined by set lists or visuals but by the feelings they leave behind. For a few magical hours, the rest of the world fades to black and white, and we are *in screaming color*.

When You Think Tim McGraw

Before headlining her own tour, Taylor spent 2007 opening for some of the biggest names in country music: Tim McGraw and Faith Hill, Rascal Flatts, George Strait, Brad Paisley, and Keith Urban. She took the stage each night to perform hits like "Our Song" and "Teardrops On My Guitar" from her debut album. Even then, she wasn't simply winning over new listeners; she was already bringing in her own. Swifties would show up early, decked out in homemade shirts and carrying glittered signs, just to catch her opening set. Some even left after her performance, having seen the one person they came for. From the start, it was clear that we were ready for Taylor to be the main event, because in our eyes, she already was.

Journey to *Fearless*

Taylor's first headlining tour was everything we'd hoped for. All you needed were cowboy boots, a hint of a country accent (even if you didn't actually have one), and a perfectly timed twirl. The crowd was a sea of Junior Jewels T-shirts and glowing lyric signs, eyes fixed on the stage, waiting for what was to come. You know that feeling you got when you first stepped into an Eras Tour stadium, or that instant sense of camaraderie during a livestream with thousands of other Swifties? As monumental as that feeling was, it was *nothing new*—the spark had already begun with this tour.

The atmosphere was unmatched, but so was Taylor's Broadway-like performance. With a castle, a staircase, and princess gowns for "Love Story," followed by theatrical elements tailored to each song, it was like walking into Taylor's imagination and watching her stories come to life for the very first time. One minute you were in a fairy tale, and the next, you were watching her throw furniture off a platform during "Forever & Always," a visual representation of heartbreak and teenage angst that gave the show its edge. There were many intimate moments throughout the tour. One was Taylor's walk through the crowd on her way to the B-stage—a second, smaller stage where she performed her acoustic set—hugging and high-fiving fans along the way.

Another came in her nightly tradition of giving her headband to a different fan, a small act that foreshadowed the kinds of fan-centered moments she would continue during future tours.

Andrea and Taylor's team would walk through the venue during the shows, searching for the most devoted fans—the ones covered in glow sticks, dancing without a care in the world, holding massive lit-up signs from the nosebleeds. Sometimes, Andrea would surprise those fans with upgraded seats closer to the stage. Other times, she'd deliver the shock of a lifetime and invite them to hang out with Taylor after the show. From then on, post-show meet and greets became a custom. For the *Fearless* Tour, it was called the T Party Room. In this case, the *T* stood for Taylor. Inside was a rainbow-colored ceiling, a Ping-Pong table, a foosball table, two large sofas, and a large column filled with tour photos, which was Taylor's favorite part of the room. Every night of the tour, a small group of fans would be invited into the T Party to spend time with Taylor and her band, friends, family, and team. Eventually, each of them would get personal one-on-one time and take photos with Taylor.

Looking back, you can see how this tour set the stage for everything that followed. The *Fearless* Tour spanned 118 shows across North America, England, Australia, and Japan, running from April 23, 2009, to July 10, 2010.

The *Speak Now* Tour

Now that we had witnessed what a Taylor Swift tour looked like, we were all eager to see where her next chapter would take us. Would it take us on another journey of love or heartbreak? Would it pull us back into a fairy tale, reigniting our imaginations as hopeless romantics? The *Speak Now* Tour captured it all, but through a lens that felt whimsical, enchanting, and extremely personal. It was intensity in the most cinematic sense: sparks flying during a kiss, letters sent to lovers, the ache of a heart you didn't mean to break, and the sweeping moments we once read about in storybooks. It embodied everything a young girl dreams about in the quiet corners of her mind—the longing, the wonder, and the wildly romantic notion that saying "I love you," even when complicated, is always worth the risk.

Taylor carried over the theatrical storytelling we'd seen on her *Fearless* Tour; however, this time, everything felt grander. Each song became even more of a full production, complete with elaborate props—like the massive bell she struck during "Haunted"—costume changes, and immersive set designs. Every detail felt intentional, each performance carefully crafted to carry the emotional weight behind the song. This tour was the more grown-up, emotionally complex version of the one before. And just as Taylor had written the *Speak Now* album entirely on her own, the tour's vision felt fully and unapologetically hers too. It was less about youthful naivete and more about a young woman realizing that life and love are layered, and that sometimes, the people we give our hearts to won't treat us the way we hoped. At its core, this tour was as much about us as it was about Taylor. The "Long Live" performance became a fan-favorite in the set list—a song capturing not only our legacy but also that of the band who had been with her since her very first headlining tour. As we sang the bridge together, we made an oath in real time, promising to stand by her forever.

During the title track, "Speak Now," Taylor wore a bridesmaid dress and stormed the stage like she was crashing a real wedding, a scene that felt straight out of a play. If I had to describe this tour in one word, it would be "captivating." The way she channeled raw vulnerability into her performances made space for us to embrace our own. Similar to the last tour, she walked through the crowd hugging fans, a reminder that even as the audience grew, she would still create ways to bring us closer.

One of my favorite traditions from that tour was Taylor writing song lyrics on her arm using a Sharpie. They changed every show, usually lines from artists she admired that resonated with her—and of course, we loved decoding the meaning behind them. Under the tour set's glowing tree, one of her standout acoustic performances was a cover of Train's "Drops of Jupiter." I don't have many regrets in life but not seeing that live definitely makes the top of the list.

A memory that lives rent-free in all of our minds is the June 25, 2011, rain show at Gillette Stadium in Foxborough, Massachusetts. Even if you weren't there, you've likely seen photos from this night. As thousands of fans sang, "With you, I'd dance in a storm in my best dress, fearless," the skies opened and rain came pouring down. Instead of dampening the moment, it fueled the stadium's energy. Fans danced harder, sang louder, and surrendered fully to the storm. Ever since, rain shows have been some of the most cherished in the fandom. Not even a downpour could dim our shine.

The T Party Room made a comeback, and Swifties continued to get handpicked by Andrea during the show. The *Speak Now* World Tour was a total of 110 shows across nineteen territories and ran from February 9, 2011, to March 18, 2012.

The *Red* Tour

Although Taylor once said she doesn't consider *Red* to be sonically cohesive, that's always been one of its greatest strengths. The album is passionate and deeply reflective. It's brave and wild in the most poetic way. It takes you on a voyage—from falling in love to believing you've found yourself to losing yourself again, falling out of love, and *beginning again*. To me, it has always felt like the truest reflection of real life, because more often than not, life doesn't feel cohesive either. When she brought *Red* to the stage, it came alive, her emotions palpable in every word.

The *Red* Tour beautifully blended Taylor's country roots with her emerging pop sound. When the curtain lifted to "State Of Grace," it set the tone for the emotional roller coaster ahead. Early in the show, we were treated to an updated version of the headband tradition, with Taylor handing her autographed hat to a lucky Swiftie. Later came the jaw-dropping "All Too Well," featuring the iconic piano hair flips—and yes, the tears.

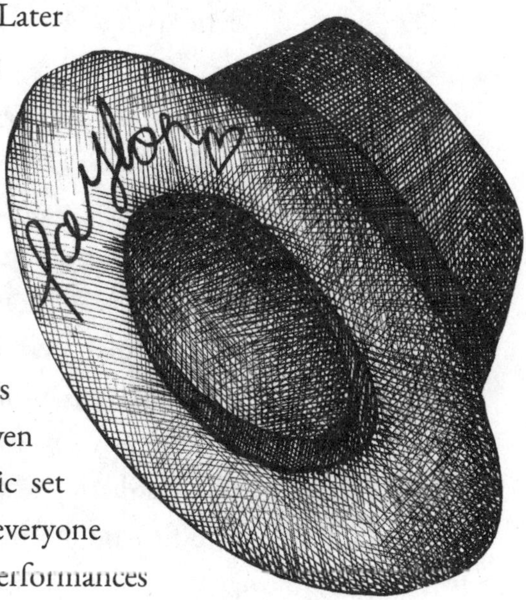

The giant U-shaped stage featured a massive runway that stretched into the crowd and two pits where fans could feel even closer to her. The acoustic set made its return, giving everyone those more stripped-back performances they looked forward to. Perhaps most importantly, this tour marked the birth of the "Sweeran" friendship, with Ed Sheeran not only collaborating with Taylor on the album but also joining her on stage as an opener.

The post-show meet and greet became known as Club Red. By this point, Taylor was one of the few artists still offering fans free ways to spend time with her. To this day, she has never made one of us pay to meet her, and what made those interactions even more meaningful was that, at times, the invitation came directly from Taylor herself.

As we all know, there was unfortunately no official film released for this tour, a tragedy we'll never recover from. The *Red* Tour kicked off on March 13, 2013, and wrapped on June 12, 2014, spanning eighty-six shows across twelve countries.

The *1989* World Tour

Oh, the *1989* Tour. This was the first tour I was ever able to see in person, and what a first it was. Following Taylor's full genre shift to pop and the explosion of her fame, this tour felt like another pivotal moment in her career. Even though it was my first Taylor concert, I went all in. I somehow convinced my parents to take me to the Massachusetts, New Jersey, and Tennessee shows—something I still can't fully wrap my head around. Unluckily for them, that decision kicked off an unbreakable habit. Truth be told, I think they were just happy to see me find something that lit me up so much. Those trips meant everything to me, and I'm forever grateful they traveled with me to those shows, especially knowing now that in the post-2022 era of ticket scalping, those kinds of experiences would've been all but impossible. This tour was when it hit me: Nowhere on earth makes me happier than a Taylor Swift concert. Forget a beach vacation—I'd rather be surrounded by thousands of Swifties, singing at the top of my lungs under the stadium lights.

From the first show, I was determined to get noticed by Taylor Nation, which led to what was both a humiliating and hilarious day in my life. Since it was the Tumblr era and Taylor followed me on there, I had what I thought was a genius idea: Come up with a concert outfit no one had ever seen before! So I ordered massive bluebird costumes online, complete with bird feet, wings, beaks, and all. Once they arrived, my mom and I tried them on, snapped photos with our poorly homemade "Bluebird Cafe" signs, and I posted them to both Tumblr and Twitter. We looked so ridiculous that, naturally, it went viral. Believe it or not, we haven't even gotten to the embarrassing part yet.

Fast-forward to our first time in Nashville. My parents and I were sitting at a restaurant on Broadway, grabbing lunch before heading to the concert venue just up the street. After eating, we slipped into the bathroom to change into our costumes. We walked in as your average mom and daughter and walked out as fully fledged bluebirds. Saying the entire restaurant stared at us would be an understatement. They were dazed, confused, and clearly not all concert-bound. My mom and I burst into uncontrollable laughter, fully aware we were being heavily judged by a large number of tourists just trying to enjoy their meals. I'm willing to bet "a couple of bluebirds emerging from the women's restroom" wasn't on their 2015 bingo cards. At least I had the excuse of being a preteen. Sorry, Mom—and thank you. Luckily, once we made it to Bridgestone Arena, we were reunited with our people. We were no longer the only ones dressed in the most extravagant outfits. Inside the venue, a man approached me and asked if I was Olivia. I said yes, and he introduced himself as someone from Taylor Nation. He told me he'd seen my costume all over Twitter that day and loved how creative it was. When he asked for our seat info, I was certain we were going to meet Taylor that night. Spoiler alert: We didn't. Of course, I was a little disappointed after getting my hopes up, but looking back, the best thing that ever happened to me was not meeting Taylor Swift while dressed as a gigantic bird.

One of the most thrilling parts of the *1989* Tour was the parade of surprise guests. From rock legends to pop stars to professional athletes, you never knew who was going to strut down the catwalk next, but you knew it'd be show-stopping. My dad, who was a fan by proxy, was ecstatic when Taylor brought out Mick Jagger to sing "(I Can't Get No) Satisfaction" and Steven Tyler for "I Don't Want to Miss a Thing" at the Nashville shows. At another show, the entire US women's soccer team came out onstage. That was the kind of unpredictable spectacle this tour delivered night after night.

I was so impressed by Taylor's stamina—not knowing she'd one day perform shows nearly twice as long. It was packed with extensive choreography, twelve backup dancers, genre-blending mash-ups, and reinvented performances, one of my favorites being the rock version of "We Are Never Ever Getting Back Together." Even her older country hits were transformed to match her new pop sound, turning this tour into a bold declaration of creative reinvention. Genre-shifting was a risky move, and not one everyone supported at first. Her label, like many, wondered: Why fix what isn't broken? But Taylor had no desire to stay in her comfort zone; she was ready for a new challenge.

Of course, the media is always the first to critique change. New hair? It looks terrible. A new sound? It's a flop. That is, until everyone starts praising it. That's simply how it goes in the world of celebrity. For fans, *1989* was a shift too, but one we were ready for. The *Red* album and tour had already helped us ease into her sonic transition, and we enjoyed every bit of it. Her willingness to evolve and take risks and her refusal to play it safe has always inspired us.

Some say pop music lacks the intimacy of country, but that's never been true for Taylor. The *1989* Tour felt just as personal as anything she's ever done. The sound may have changed, but the depth of her lyrics never did. The "Clean" speech from this tour remains one of her most enduring pieces of wisdom, one we still find ourselves quoting often.

Loft '89 became the official post-show meet and greet for the *1989* Tour. By then Taylor's fame—and her relationship with us—had evolved tremendously. With the rise of social media and her daily interactions with us on Tumblr, we were in constant conversation with her. It was also the era when she had started welcoming us into her homes for the first-ever Secret Sessions, making it a thrilling time to be a Swiftie!

This tour kicked off several new fan traditions. A signature highlight came during the bridge of "Blank Space," when fans during every tour stop would harmonize with Taylor, shouting the name of their city in unison. Since the *1989* Tour film was shot at ANZ Stadium in Sydney, Australia, many of us still yell "Sydney!" no matter what city we're actually in. Another fan-made addition was shouting, "You forgive, you forget, but you never let it go!" during the "Bad Blood" bridge, which was our collective way of filling in Kendrick Lamar's part on the remix.

It no longer felt like we were watching a girl still searching for her place. Instead, we were witnessing someone who had collected stories from new cities, new friendships, and new heartbreaks, but returned with a stronger sense of self. Taylor shared her hard-earned truths with us and this time it was from a place of clarity and growth. Even so, more growth was still on the horizon. The *1989* World Tour began on May 5, 2015, and concluded on December 12, 2015, after eighty-five shows across eleven countries.

The *Reputation* Stadium Tour

Setting my own bias aside, anyone who went to the *Reputation* Tour could feel how different it was from the others. It came after millions had flooded Taylor's comments sections with snake emojis and written her career off, followed by her vanishing from the spotlight for over a year. 2016 meant constantly defending her name every time she came up in conversation. We knew she was in the right, but the damage to her reputation had already been done. Just as she had fair-weather friends, she had fair-weather fans. Some walked away, likely never having been fully invested to begin with. The real ones stayed.

As a result, this tour felt like a high school reunion, filled with your closest Swiftie friends and online mutuals. I went to the shows in Massachusetts, New Jersey, Tennessee, and Ohio. Ticketmaster had a surprisingly fan-friendly system for this tour. All we had to do to boost our place in line for tickets was watch Taylor's AT&T cookie dough commercial—yes, that one with Andy Samberg. It was a silly but effective way to make sure real fans had a fair shot at purchasing tickets. Sure, the demand wasn't quite what it would be for the next tour, but even then she was still selling out stadiums.

For the *Rep* Tour, Taylor brought back the walk through the crowd from one B-stage to the other, which felt like her way of saying, "Thank you for still being here." One of my favorite memories was the mad dash to the barricade near the B-stage during "King Of My Heart," two songs before she'd make her way over to perform "Shake It Off." It became a ritual among the online Swifties. We'd rush over, breathless and excited, recognizing each other in the crowd and yelling, "Oh my God, hi!" between the politest (but absolutely necessary) shoves. Those who had met Taylor before would hold up enlarged photos of their encounters—some dating back to 2006; others like mine from just the year before. It was as if our little corner of the internet had come to life.

No matter what show I was at, it became tradition for me to carry around an eight-by-ten-inch print of the photo Taylor and I took at her house. I brought it, hoping Taylor would see it and be reminded that we were still there, supporting her. At one show, my friends and I made it to the barricade right before her walk down the heavily secured aisle. I was filming with one hand and holding up the photo with the other, hoping she'd catch a glimpse. Of course, right before she reached me, the universe had other plans. My phone stopped recording and a dreaded "your storage is full" notification popped up on the screen. *God, I'm an idiot*, I thought. Why didn't I clear my phone before the show? The answer was simple: I was always at Taylor Swift concerts, and my storage was already full . . . of other Taylor Swift concerts. It didn't matter, though; my plan still worked! Taylor saw the photo, smiled big, and waved at me. She's always had this uncanny ability to find familiar faces in the crowd, and you could tell how much she appreciated those who kept showing up—especially in this era, when so many had turned away.

Let's not forget that this was the tour when "1, 2, 3, let's go, bitch!" was born, thanks to a Swiftie who shouted it during "Delicate" and posted the video online. It went so viral that others started doing it too. Until one day, Taylor began counting the "1, 2, 3" with her fingers, fully embracing the new practice. It's safe to say we'll be doing it at every tour for the rest of time. Another viral moment came when a fan screamed "Take me to church!" just before Taylor hit that chill-inducing high note in "Don't Blame Me." Soon, many of us began dropping to our knees and screaming it from the stadiums' dirty floors. At the time, one of my online friends' mom even dressed up as a priest to honor the stunning bridge. I can only imagine the confusion of any casual fans who happened to be there.

Once again, Taylor carried on her post-show meet and greets, this time calling it Rep Room. At first, Taylor Nation had in place a rule that you could be chosen to meet her only once—a decision that sparked plenty of online frustration from fans who had met her a decade earlier and desperately wanted another opportunity. Eventually the rule softened, allowing fans to meet her once per era, or after they deemed that enough time had passed. With each Rep Room invitation, timelines filled with Swifties swapping their profile pictures for photos with Taylor. She prioritized meeting those of us she knew from online, showing love to the ones who had stuck with her through the trenches. I'll always remember being at one of the Ohio shows and seeing a girl I knew get chosen during the concert; she fell to her knees and sobbed.

In so many ways, this tour was a reunion between an artist and her most devoted, lifelong fans. The *Reputation* Stadium Tour ran from May 8 to November 21, 2018, spanning fifty-three shows across seven countries—and it certainly left a lasting impression on all of us.

I See Your Face in Every Crowd

What came next was supposed to be *Lover* Fest—a pastel-pink-drenched dream of a tour that never saw *daylight*. I was in college and ecstatic that I had gotten pit tickets for one of the shows. But like so many things in 2020, it was canceled due to the global pandemic. Still, this album would get its time to shine at the Eras Tour, where "Cruel Summer" became the smash hit it always deserved to be, four years after its release.

Our journey has taken us from cafés to packed arenas, and from arenas to sold-out stadiums. No matter the size of the crowd, the shows always kept their same sense of connection, and it always felt like Taylor was singing directly to us right when we needed it most. Without these tours, and without us showing up again and again, we wouldn't be where we are today as a fandom. As the final confetti floated to the ground and the stage lights came up, it felt less like an ending and more like a pause, a breath before the biggest tour of them all began.

More than a celebration of past eras, the Eras Tour became a cultural phenomenon that created an era of its own—one that transformed more than just Taylor's life. Her stardom skyrocketed, and with it, our community grew immensely. Swifties had always been present, but suddenly all eyes were on us.

CHAPTER EIGHT

Welcome to the Eras Tour

It's a beautiful Saturday, and the air is electric with anticipation as seventy-five thousand people gather. Children and adults are trading friendship bracelets with complete strangers as if it's the most natural introduction in the world. Hugs abound, and everyone's smiling at one another. As I walk through and take it all in, I realize this might be the closest thing to pure joy many of us will ever experience. For the first time in my life, watching this massive crowd beaming with love and light, hate feels like a foreign concept.

As I keep watching, I see a group of fans running up to each other, throwing their arms around one another. One is dressed in Taylor's classic Junior Jewels tee from the "You Belong With Me" music video, while the others are sporting various looks from "Shake It Off." It feels like the biggest Halloween party, and

I'm wearing my own sparkly rendition of one of Taylor's iconic Debut era outfits. I make my way over to say hi to the group I've been watching, and before I even have a chance to speak, one of them screams, "Olivia!" For a moment, I'm surprised, before I realize she knows me from my @swiftiesforeternity account. A rush of warmth floods me, and I can't help but grin from ear to ear. For nearly two hours during the preshow, I mingle with other Swifties, swapping stories as if we're old friends reunited after years apart. I'm overwhelmed with gratitude.

After hours spent talking, laughing, and waiting in what feels like endless merch lines, Taylor is about to take the stage. The stadium feels alive, pulsing with collective energy as our heartbeats move in sync, all fueled by a shared admiration for the woman whose music has captured our hearts. The cheers are so loud that no earplugs could block out the noise. While many of us are veterans from previous tours, many are here for the very first time, and we couldn't be happier to welcome them. The crowd spans every generation, from children to adults to grandparents, and is made up of nearly as many men as women. The idea that Taylor Swift is only for young girls is long gone. Now, being a Taylor Swift fan is for everyone.

Finally, after years of counting down the days until we'd see our idol sing live again, the night we've dreamed of is here. All eyes are on the clock displayed on the giant screen as the crowd begins counting down the seconds. When it clicks to midnight, the screams are deafening. The screen lights up, piece by piece, revealing different-colored rooms that represent the different eras we're about to experience. In the background, Taylor's voice echoes each album title, sending shivers down our spines. We know the significance of it all. The number thirteen, the countdown to midnight, the various colors—they're the secret language that bonds us.

Now dancers move gracefully down the catwalk, carrying enormous parachutes billowing above their heads in the sunset pastels of the *Lover* era. They bend forward, meeting in the middle, and when they rise, Taylor Swift is standing there. And just like that, all is right in the world again.

It Was Rare, We Were There

This was her longest and most groundbreaking tour yet. Families grew closer. Friends gathered. Swiftie influencers emerged. Millions of friendship bracelets were traded. Not to be dramatic, but lives were changed, mine included. My online community grew beyond anything I could have ever imagined, and I was able to turn being a Swiftie from just my passion into something more. For all of us, it was the tour that cemented Taylor's icon status, shattered countless records, and ensured that *we will be remembered*.

Every single city on the Eras Tour was unique in its own way. Philadelphia was when Taylor yelled "Hey, stop!" at the security guard for being too aggressive with a fan during "Bad Blood." Nashville was the *Speak Now (Taylor's Version)* announcement and the monsoon that forced fans to shelter in place for nearly four hours. Taylor still performed once the thunder and lightning advisory was lifted, wrapping the show at 1:30 a.m. It was also there that the Centennial Park bench was placed in her honor—

a lasting tribute in the city where her story began. Foxborough, Massachusetts, had the second most intense rain show, with the video of Taylor pushing pools of water off her piano going viral. The very next night featured the *haunted* piano, playing entirely on its own due to it being "underwater" the night before. Kansas City was Taylor Lautner doing flips onstage and the release of the "I Can See You (Taylor's Version)" music video. The city also carried the energy of a new beginning as Taylor smiled and asked that very special audience, "Would you allow me the honor of starting over?" Los Angeles was the infamous blue dress and the *1989 (Taylor's Version)* announcement. Buenos Aires was that kiss after Taylor ran offstage. Rio de Janeiro was Taylor ripping off her broken Christian Louboutin heel and tossing it to a fan, who later auctioned it off to help his cousin pay for cancer treatment. But it was also Taylor's Junior Jewels shirt being projected onto the Christ the Redeemer statue. Paris brought the debut of *The Tortured Poets Department* set. London was Travis Kelce dressing up as a backup dancer and resuscitating Taylor onstage. Munich was fifty-two thousand people watching from the hill overlooking the stadium, and in that moment, she truly had *the whole place surrounded*. The one thing every city had in common? The clowning for a *reputation (Taylor's Version)* announcement.

Then there was Vienna, perhaps the most memorable city of all. You could write an entire book just about this tour—and Taylor already did. But no story of ours is complete without it, which revealed the true scale, spirit, and devotion of our community.

The Eras Tour was far more than a tour. It was a two-year journey through every chapter of Taylor's life and career, taking us back to times where her songs first found us, and carrying us forward into new eras of our own lives at the same time. Each leg of the tour unfolded like a mini-chapter in a saga larger than life itself. Before revisiting them, we must go back to where it all started. Like many great stories, it began in mayhem.

"The Great War"

We will never forget the day Ticketmaster canceled the general sale, revealing that nearly all Eras Tour tickets had already sold in the presale. There's a reason we call it "The Great War." I was walking down the streets of Florida while on vacation with my family when I saw the announcement. "What?!" I shouted. My mom asked what was wrong. "There are no more tickets. I'm so confused. How did they miscalculate how many tickets they could sell? How is everyone going to get tickets?" I said, staring at my phone in disbelief. This was new territory for us. Before this, we never had issues securing tickets to Taylor's shows—or any concert, for that matter. I had personally never paid more than $300 to see her, and those were usually front-row floor seats. Immediately, I worried that my family and I wouldn't be able to go see her together like we always did, but more than that, I was heartbroken for the people who had never seen her live and had been waiting for this moment their entire lives.

Due to the cancellation of *Lover* Fest, we had all patiently waited five years for her to tour again. Social media became a disaster zone, flooded with devastated fans. Amid the storm, scalpers realized just how valuable these tickets were, and prices surged overnight. Tickets that were originally listed on Ticketmaster for $150 suddenly appeared on StubHub for $5,000. The most insane part of all this? Fans were buying them, which only fueled the scalpers. Still, I understood. For many of us, seeing her perform live was priceless. Concert ticketing has always had its flaws, but nothing compared to this. Following that day, purchasing concert tickets was never the same. The incident ignited such outrage that even Congress got involved—but more on that later. Despite it all, one thing was clear: Nothing, not even ticket scalpers, could stop us from showing up for Taylor.

At the start of the tour, my followers began messaging me, asking for help selling their extra tickets to other fans. They wanted to make sure their tickets went to someone deserving, a true Swiftie, not someone who would just turn around and resell them for profit. The more I posted tickets, the more sellers came forward. For nearly the first year and a half of the tour, I did this every single day. Eventually, there were so many submissions that I couldn't keep up, so I created a Google Form for sellers, which made it easier to stay organized and quickly spot scammers. In the final months of the tour, I partnered with a subscription platform that allowed me to dedicate entire workdays to helping fans experience the tour before its grand finale. I started early and spent long hours each day sifting through submissions, verifying tickets, and messaging with buyers and sellers. It was an honor to help connect fans who thought they might never get the chance to go—an effort made possible only by other fans willing to pass their tickets on at face value.

Some of my favorite stories were born from this. One was a

mom and her young daughter who decided to take a road trip to Miami in hopes of a miracle. She wrote that they had their outfits and friendship bracelets ready to go, but no concert tickets. They were still on their way when I messaged the mom to tell her she and her daughter were going to the Eras Tour that night. She told me it was the best day of her life, along with a video of her sharing the news with her daughter. Another one that stuck with me was when a husband wanted to surprise his wife. He was a US veteran and hoped to buy just one ticket for her. After being selected, he bought the ticket, booked her a flight for the next day, and surprised her. She went to the show alone and had the time of her life.

The hardest part was not being able to help everyone. There were so many parents wanting to take their kids, and fans hoping to surprise their best friends. It was absolutely heart-wrenching, and I only wished everyone could have gone, because everyone deserved to.

The Very First Night

The tour kicked off on March 17, 2023, in Glendale, Arizona. For that weekend, the mayor officially renamed Glendale as "Swift City," making it the first of many cities to change their names in Taylor's honor. No one knew exactly what to expect from the first show, but thousands of us flew in to witness it, knowing it would be nothing short of spectacular.

How could she possibly fit all the eras in so seamlessly? Her discography was so massive that everyone assumed we'd get only a couple of songs from each album. If it were anyone else, that's most likely how it would have gone. But this was Taylor Swift we were talking about, and if anyone could pull off the impossible, it was her. Even though there were nearly seventy thousand people in attendance, it seemed like the entire Swiftie universe was there, brought together by livestreams and social media updates. In the hours leading up to the first show, I remember a photo circulating online of a piece of paper that claimed the concert would run for three and a half hours. No one believed it. There was just no way. By 11:30 p.m. millions of jaws were on the floor, and forty-four songs, fifteen backup dancers, and a flurry of outfit changes later, the first show had come to an end.

Setting the Stage

The Eras Tour wasn't just about the music; it was a full-scale production, so immersive that it carried us through a story that spanned decades, one era at a time. With countless set pieces—from the willow trees to the glass cages in the *reputation* section, where dancers portrayed the "old Taylors," to the *folklore* cabin—each era of the show felt like entering another universe. The stage itself stretched across the stadium in a massive T-shape, with a runway that seemed to go on forever. From the crowd, Taylor looked larger than life. But from her perspective, as her favorite backup dancer once described it, standing on that vast stage made you feel like "the smallest piece of life," as tiny as an ant.

Even the behind-the-scenes details had their own quirks,

such as the famous mop cart. Before each show, Taylor would be wheeled to the stage inside it—a not-so-subtle disguise that instantly became a joke among fans. The second the cart appeared, we knew it was showtime. Only Taylor could turn something as ordinary as a cleaning cart into something we'd look back on fondly.

One of the most surprising nights of the tour came when a brand-new album, *The Tortured Poets Department*, was added to the set list during the very first show of the European leg. During the newly added set, a standout scene unfolded as she floated across the stage on what fans labeled the "Tayoomba"—a moving platform used during "Who's Afraid of Little Old Me?" Of course, we didn't know at the time that while she was living *the life of a showgirl*, she was already drawing on it as inspiration for her next era—proof that no one works harder than Taylor Swift.

It wasn't only Taylor's immaculate storytelling onstage that made the shows epic; we played our part too. In several cities, the glowing orbs project transformed whole sections of the audience into a shimmering light display. Thousands of glowing orbs lit up in unison, with fans even joining Taylor in the "willow" choreography. Taylor herself laughed about it onstage: "There have been people bringing balloons to the Eras Tour to make their own orbs for 'willow.' I was cracking up the whole time. You guys are so thoughtful." And at the final show of the entire Eras Tour on December 8, 2024, just days before Taylor's thirty-fifth birthday, Swifties organized a surprise singalong, replacing the usual extended applause after "champagne problems" with a heartfelt chorus of "Happy Birthday."

Our Secret Moments in a Crowded Room

During the Eras Tour, we carried on our traditions from the earlier tours, making sure the newer fans learned them too, and together we created new ones. Entire stadiums of ninety-six thousand people now knew exactly when to chant "1, 2, 3, let's go, bitch" during "Delicate," when to do the two claps in "You Belong With Me," shout "Taylor, you'll be fine" in "Anti-Hero," add the three claps in "Shake It Off," cheer for as many minutes as possible after "champagne problems" (with the longest applause lasting about eight minutes), and scream "Karma is the guy on the *Chiefs*," among countless others. Taylor even joined in sometimes, giving us little hand signals to cue the chants. Yet there's one moment we all remember that wasn't planned at all: when she sang "Exile" as a surprise song and the entire stadium of Swifties became her duet partner, harmonizing with her in Bon Iver's absence. It was breathtaking.

Our culture even extended to fan-made artifacts, like when Barstool Sports' Dave Portnoy wore what eventually became known as "the traveling Eras jacket." After he showed up to a concert in the hand-painted denim jacket—designed with all ten eras—it began its own journey, passed on from city to city. Each Swiftie who wore it added their own touch, spritzing it with their perfume before sending it along, until the jacket carried a mingling of scents—a living patchwork of the people and places it had passed through. An Instagram account, @daveserasjacket, started documenting its travels early on, turning it into a fan-favorite storyline to follow. By the end, the jacket had become a symbol of the tour itself, a piece of clothing cherished by fans across the world.

While some fans traveled to stadiums to partake in the "Taygates" even without tickets, perhaps the most important Eras Tour tradition was tuning in to the online livestreams of the shows. It was reminiscent of how we used to chat on Tumblr during past tours, only now we had more advanced technology. As the tour went on, fans generously streamed from their concert seats, letting Swifties everywhere tune in on YouTube, TikTok, and Instagram. Every single weekend, without fail, we made the Eras Tour trend across social media. Yet what really made it accessible to everyone was the Swiftfluencers, who shared those links and broadcasted the streams to their followers, making sure no one missed out. It completely changed the way we "attended" concerts. Fans also leaned in to the Swift Alert app, turning each show into a game of predictions. We'd guess everything from which surprise songs Taylor would sing to what color outfits she'd wear, a nightly ritual that brought us even closer together as a fandom. For the overwhelming number of us who weren't lucky enough to get tickets, it became the perfect way to be virtually present and still feel connected.

During the surprise song set, there would always be a massive influx of viewers: First, everyone wanted to see which songs she would sing and what creative mash-ups she'd come up with. Second, just in case she announced something important—like a new re-record or a new music video. And third, to catch any potential surprise guests she might bring out, like Gracie Abrams or Sabrina Carpenter. Few things caused more dramatic (yet justified) reactions online than not being there in person for your ultimate surprise song or special guest appearance. When Taylor performed "You're On Your Own, Kid" live for the first time, everyone immediately started posting "RIP me. Died. Dead." memes about it. That is, until it thankfully became a surprise-song regular.

In so many ways, the Eras Tour felt like the ultimate group-therapy session . . . and group project. Swifties wore the most creative, extravagant outfits, many of them handmade, each showcasing unique artistic abilities. Above all, we showed up to scream the words that continued to carry us through our lives. Somehow, by the end of each night, we all walked out a little lighter. After several hours of dancing and singing, our bodies may have been exhausted, but emotionally, we had never felt more awake.

Midnight Rain

In May 2023, I went to the Eras Tour with my mom. Now, it's a Sunday night, and we're road-tripping from Connecticut to my personal favorite stadium, Gillette. Taylor's music fills the car as flashes of our one special trip to Rhode Island flicker through my mind. Outside, rain lashes the windshield in a torrential downpour. Nothing excites me more than finally getting to experience a Taylor Swift rain show. We park about a mile from the stadium and begin walking toward the venue where we last saw her together during the *Reputation* Tour in 2018. The outfit I've so carefully planned disappears beneath my poncho, and any hope of cute photos is gone. It doesn't matter. Seeing Taylor with my mom is my favorite tradition.

We arrive at the stadium and join the merch line. It snakes around the inside of the building and looks at least half a mile long, but that doesn't stop us. I'm on a mission to snag the blue crewneck that sent us all into a frenzy for no real reason—classic Swiftie herd mentality. While we wait, we trade bracelets and stories with the people around us. Nearly two hours later, we finally reach the front and ask for the blue crewneck. Only one size is left, but I grab it anyway, along with a few shirts for my brother and his boyfriend. Before heading to our seats, we fuel up for the three-and-a-half-hour show and map out a bathroom strategy so we won't miss a single second. On the way to my floor seat, I bump into a girl I met at Taylor's house back in 2017. We haven't talked in years, but there's an instant sense of familiarity from that night we shared. We try to snap a selfie, but it's still pouring rain and our mascara is fighting for its life. After catching up for a few minutes, we're ushered to our seats for the openers.

Phoebe Bridgers takes the stage. I know some of her music but not all of it, yet as she performs her eight-song set I'm struck by her talent. I'm grateful to Taylor for giving women like Phoebe a platform to shine before seventy-nine thousand people who, like me, will inevitably fall in love with their music. That's how it started for me—with Phoebe, Gracie, Sabrina, and so many others.

At last, "In Ha Mood" by Ice Spice blasts through the stadium, and with the first beat drop the crowd roars. Those paying attention know the countdown is about eight minutes away. The rain is now heavier than anything I've ever stood in, and our ponchos are useless; we look like we just climbed out of a pool. But we're so giddy it doesn't even phase us.

"Applause" by Lady Gaga comes on as everyone rushes back to their seats after last-minute bathroom and merch runs. Two minutes pass, and the final preshow track begins: "You Don't Own

Me" by Lesley Gore. *What a statement*, I think. Right before performing songs from her entire life's work—some of which were taken away from her—she makes sure everyone in the stadium understands one thing: She isn't owned by anyone.

The clock appears. The countdown begins. Rain keeps pouring down as my mom and I look at each other and just smile.

Celebrities Are Swifties Too

As we all know, the Eras Tour became the talk of every town. The number of celebrities who revealed themselves as Swifties during this tour was astronomical. No one was too cool to attend a show; in fact, being there became somewhat of a status symbol. Athletes, actors, singers, and their families all showed up to experience it. Just to give you an idea of the range, here are a few of the many celebrities who had the time of their lives:

- Tom Brady
- J. J. Watt
- Aaron Rodgers
- Serena Williams
- Travis Kelce
- Patrick Mahomes & Brittany Mahomes
- Mariska Hargitay
- Ellen Pompeo
- Reese Witherspoon
- Nicole Kidman
- Keith Urban

- Flavor Flav
- Zoë Kravitz
- Marcus Mumford
- Paul Rudd
- Sofia Vergara
- Gigi Hadid
- Bradley Cooper
- Kevin Costner
- Tom Cruise
- Hugh Grant
- Emma Stone
- Haim (sisters Este, Danielle & Alana)
- Charlize Theron
- Paula Abdul
- Paul McCartney
- Selena Gomez
- Stevie Nicks
- Shania Twain
- Alicia Keys
- Katy Perry
- Hayley Williams
- Emma Watson
- Jennifer Garner
- Brooke Shields
- Paul Mescal
- Gordon Ramsay
- Julia Roberts
- Cate Blanchett
- Ellie Goulding

- Jack Antonoff & Margaret Qualley
- Max Martin
- Billy Joel
- Hugh Jackman
- Prince William, Prince George & Princess Charlotte
- Greta Gerwig

Throughout the tour, I became online mutuals with several celebrity Swifties, including Alyson Hannigan, Noah Kahan, and Nikki Glaser. Alyson, an actress best known for her roles in *How I Met Your Mother* and *American Pie*, was someone I even had the pleasure of chatting with periodically.

Alyson proudly joined the Swiftie ranks during the Eras Tour. She'd always loved Taylor's music but never felt she truly "earned the title" of Swiftie until then. Her gateway into the fandom was *Miss Americana*, which she watched during the pandemic. The documentary showed her a side of Taylor she hadn't seen before—someone levelheaded and humble, not just a brilliant songwriter. During lockdown, *folklore* and *evermore* became a lifeline. Alyson remembers sitting in her car in the driveway, listening to both albums straight through while her kids were on Zoom for school inside. "I just don't know if there's any other public figure I respect more," she said.

It was the Eras Tour that sealed the deal. When Alyson went to the LA show with her daughters, they had no idea about the friendship bracelet tradition. While waiting in line for the bathroom behind a woman dressed like a princess, someone asked if they had bracelets to trade. Her daughters were too shy to accept one at first, but by the end of the night their arms were covered.

Alyson said, "It was like watching a fashion show just seeing everyone's outfits. And then inside, it felt like this beautiful community of love, with seventy thousand people all feeling connected." By the time the last song ended, there was no doubt left: Alyson was a forever Swiftie.

She later went to the Eras Tour's final show in Vancouver and was struck by Taylor's work ethic and humility—how she never called it "my tour," always acknowledging and thanking her dancers, crew, and everyone who made it possible. "It was next-level . . . I didn't realize how sad I was going to feel when it ended. I was genuinely heartbroken," Alyson told me. The next morning at the airport, she had an unexpected moment of connection. While waiting in the security line, she noticed a man ahead of her who looked like a heavy-metal rocker in a ripped denim jacket. When someone asked if he worked on the tour, he nodded. He was part of the pyrotechnics team. As he spoke about how sad he was that it was over, tears streamed down his face. Alyson handed him a packet of tissues and one of her friendship bracelets—prompting another wave of tears. "He told us Taylor is the most generous person he's ever met," she said, likely referring to the large bonuses Taylor gave to everyone who worked on the tour.

Alyson also appeared on *Dancing with the Stars* during Taylor Swift night, something she called her ultimate goal on the show. "I thought, there's no way I'll make it to that week, but if I do, I'll feel like I've won," she said. Before the taping, she ordered and made hundreds of friendship bracelets to hand out to the audience.

When I asked about her favorite Taylor album, she said, "It changes every day," before adding that "'So High School' has to be my favorite song now because Taylor mentions *American Pie*."

Alyson laughed. "I was in that movie!" But for Alyson, the Eras Tour wasn't just about the music. It was about bonding with her daughters, feeling the love of the community, and watching an artist who had remained grounded despite so many people giving her reasons not to be. "It didn't take her down, it just made her better," she said. "It's such a cool community. We need more of that in the world."

Eras Tour Journal Entries

2/16/24—MELBOURNE NIGHT ONE

Taylor's second tour stop of 2024 was last night in Melbourne, Australia, which means my sleep schedule is officially gone. I went to bed at 10 p.m. and woke up at 3 a.m. to join a livestream, posting on Instagram as much as I could until my eyes shut. It didn't really matter, though—I had already set a 5 a.m. alarm for the surprise songs. For the first time on this tour, we got a mash-up of multiple songs, and everyone online was losing it. After posting about it, I stayed up just long enough to watch her dive into the stage, making sure there weren't any unexpected announcements or plot twists.

We've been clowning for REPUTATION (TAYLOR'S VERSION) for what feels like forever, but something tells me it won't come until the end of the tour, or maybe even next year. Either way, I'm always ready to post about a new REPUTATION outfit or an album announcement at a moment's notice. After years of decoding her cryptic easter eggs, we've become hypersensitive to her ways. You can't blame us—SHE TRAINED US. Once the surprise songs were over, I fell back asleep, knowing this would be my routine for the rest of the international leg. Honestly, it's nothing I haven't done before. And it's exactly what international Swifties had already been doing, gracefully, while Taylor was touring the US.

10/18/24—MIAMI NIGHT ONE

Months have passed without an Eras Tour show since the European leg wrapped in London. Even though we hope it'll never come to an end, we all know the finale is near. Miami marks the first stop of the last three US cities, with New Orleans and Indianapolis still to come.

I was recently a guest on Barstool Sports' TAYLOR WATCH podcast and got to know the hosts, Kelly and Gia. They ended up meeting me in Miami and are staying at my Airbnb. Once again, our online Swiftie community has turned strangers into friends. It reminded me of the time I flew to Ohio for those REPUTATION Tour shows all those years ago.

Miami's first night was incredible, if a little chaotic. I ended up getting a last-minute ticket from a friend who had an extra one, and then Kelly, Gia, and I headed to the stadium. When we arrived, Gia spent hours in the merch line, which stretched around the inside of the stadium. She already owned all the Taylor merch but really wanted the brown Gracie Abrams hoodie. While she waited in line, Kelly and I wandered around, eagerly

searching for food and trying to fuel up for the long night ahead. At one point, a girl came up to us while we were getting drinks and started screaming "Oh my God!" over and over. Finally, she said, "I've followed you on Instagram for so long!" and then turned to Kelly and said, "And I love your podcast!" She was so sweet and pure. There's no better place to make new friends than at a Taylor concert. The preshow moments of talking, taking photos, and exchanging bracelets in the stadium hallways may seem small, but they're the little wonders that make the tour so unforgettable.

It was more than the stereotypical Swifties filling the stadium. Directly in front of me sat four frat-looking guys in their twenties. They had traveled all the way from Boston because one of them loved Taylor's music. His friends were so supportive, sneaking little glances his way as if to make sure he was having the time of his life. They filmed him, took photos of him with Taylor in the background, and at one point two of them threw their arms around him while singing along. They were wearing friendship bracelets too, and one of the boys slipped one onto the wrist of an older woman nearby who looked like she was there alone. It was the cutest thing I'd ever seen. A few seats over, someone was FaceTiming their friend during what was clearly their favorite song. Everywhere I turned, I saw people embracing the best versions of themselves, free from judgment. I remember thinking this stadium was the only place where true ALCHEMY existed—where authenticity and joy seemed infinite and a mutual gratitude for that very moment radiated through every corner of the crowd.

"AHHHHH! NEW REPUTATION BODYSUIT!" I screamed as Taylor strutted out during ". . . Ready For It?" This was the first time the REPUTATION set had gotten a new outfit, and it was huge news. Was REPUTATION (TAYLOR'S VERSION) coming soon? Was she just teasing us as usual?

Had she simply grown tired of the old one? What may seem inconsequential to someone else can hold great meaning for us. And even though I was at the show, I was still on the clock. If something big happened, I wanted to be the first to share it with the online Swifties. Thankfully, the Hard Rock Stadium internet service was on my side, which was rarely the case in any stadium. As Taylor kept singing, I quickly uploaded a video of the new bodysuit on Instagram. To say people were ecstatic would be the understatement of the century. We were crashing out.

As if that wasn't enough, Florence Welch came out as a surprise guest to sing "Florida!!!" with Taylor, which in and of itself felt like an out-of-body experience. IN THE BLINK OF A CRINKLING EYE, night one in Miami had come to a close.

10/20/24—MIAMI NIGHT THREE

I woke up early this morning to do an interview with a French news station that came to my Airbnb, still feeling my Eras Tour show hangover from the night before. They're filming a documentary on the impact of the Eras Tour airing in France next week. As a half-French girl, I'm beyond excited for this opportunity, and I know my family in Paris will appreciate seeing me on their screens, even if they still have a hard time understanding everything that goes into the Swiftie experience. I often try to explain it, and they'll respond with something like, "Why don't you just call Taylor?" A line I'm sure many of us have heard from older generations.

After the interview, I headed to Hollywood to meet up with my mom before taking the Taylor-themed Brightline train to the stadium. Several familiar faces were on the train, including Gloria Estefan—such an icon. As we were getting off, I ran into Zachery (better known on Instagram as @mdmotivator), who I had previously interacted with a *bit online. He's the guy who films videos of himself giving money and opportunities to people in need. I said hi, and he told me he was bringing a little girl named Mia to the concert and was hoping to get her the "22" hat. Knowing about my account, he asked if I could help. I said I couldn't guarantee anything, but if I put it out on social media, there was always a chance the right eyes would see it.*

When we got to the stadium, Zach and I asked a concession stand for a cardboard box and a pen. We tore it up and made a sign that said, "22 days out of cancer era . . . now in my Rep era," crammed into the little room we had. I posted a photo of all of us holding the sign and tagged Taylor Nation. It went viral across every platform almost instantly, but unfortunately, there wasn't enough time for them to see it before the show started. Even so, Mia still had one of the greatest nights of her life.

Soon after, I ran into Jackson Olson—you might know him from the Savannah Bananas baseball team . . . or TikTok. We'd actually become friends online through the simple fact that we were both Swifties, and so many people kept tagging us in each other's content. We filmed a quick video together, once again proving that Taylor Swift and sports make the ultimate duo.

I ended the night with my mom as we headed up to our seats in the nosebleeds, watching the show from the second-to-last row of the stadium. No matter where you sit, you're guaranteed to have a breathtaking view, surrounded by thousands of other people who know every word just like you do. There's no feeling quite like it.

11/2/24—INDIANAPOLIS NIGHT TWO

I flew in from LA last night to meet up with a friend in Indianapolis. Today, we went to several Eras Tour–themed events and met tons of Swifties—some recognizing us from social media. Even though we weren't going to the show, we strolled around the stadium, striking up conversations with fans, and that's when we met a woman named Susan. She was sitting alone in a shimmering outfit. We both asked if we could take a photo of it, and she smiled and said, "Of course!" before turning around to show the back of her jacket. It read, "In my cancer survivor era."

She told us she was hoping for a ticket miracle. She had tickets for the Eras Tour earlier that summer but ended up selling them to another fan because she got sick. Her story moved me, and I knew I had to find a way to get her into that stadium. She wasn't sure if she'd be staying the entire weekend, so before we left, I said, "Make sure you come back to this spot tomorrow."

I shared her story on Instagram, and it spread like wildfire. A girl messaged me saying she had an extra ticket for the next day's show because her cousin had bailed. I filled her in on Susan's story and arranged to meet her before the next show. An incredibly generous Swiftie joined me in putting up the money to buy the ticket. Knowing it would be my last time near an Eras Tour stadium, helping a fellow Swiftie's dream come true felt destined.

11/3/24—INDIANAPOLIS NIGHT THREE

Today was the day Susan would finally get to see the Eras Tour. I woke up early and spent the morning organizing every detail to make sure nothing went wrong. After getting ready, we headed to the stadium. As we approached, we found Susan sitting in the exact same place as the day before. We hid from her so we could find the girl who had the ticket. Finally, we found her and her friends. They were all wearing matching shirts that said "Sam," "Sophia," and "Marcus," but they were missing their "Chloe." As we walked over to Susan together, the girls began chanting "Chloe!" and I joined in. She looked completely confused, understandably so, because her name wasn't Chloe.

When we reached her, I said, "You're going to be watching the Eras Tour tonight from a really great floor seat." The shock and sheer happiness on her face made my entire year. She was overwhelmed, having one of those moments where you wonder if life is even real. "These girls are going to be sitting with you, and they have a 'Chloe' shirt for you if you want to be part of their group," I added. Tears streamed down her face as she put on the shirt and took a photo with them. We hugged for what felt like ten minutes. It was DEFINITELY THE HIGHLIGHT OF MY ERAS TOUR YEAR.

During the show, I received a text from Susan:

Top 4 nights of my life:
1. Birth of my oldest son
2. Birth of my twins
3. The night my boyfriend of 13 years kissed me for the first time
4. Right now. This moment. Tonight.

Bigger Than The Whole Sky

The Vienna, Austria, shows were scheduled for August 8–10, 2024, but were canceled at the last minute due to a terrorist threat that would have put everyone in the stadium at risk. Still, those dates remain among the most precious of the entire tour.

Rain or shine, sick or healthy, Taylor never cancels a show. So when she did, we knew it had to be for a truly serious reason and that her hands were tied. She'd always been terrified of something like the Manchester Arena bombing happening again—and honestly, so were we. As Taylor said, though, thankfully we were grieving concerts, not lives. Thousands of fans had flown in from all over for the Vienna shows. I knew several people who landed on the runway only to discover the shows had been canceled, and I was devastated for everyone whose weekend was now in shambles. We all were.

I was getting hundreds of messages from Swifties who were scared, had traveled solo, and now didn't know what to do in Vienna. I shared these messages on Instagram, and almost instantly,

other Swifties began reaching out, inviting them to spend time with their groups while there. One person messaged me saying, "I came to Vienna alone and am now just hanging out in my hotel room, not feeling like sleeping, with dozens of friendship bracelets and nobody to exchange them with." I ended up connecting her with another woman, who offered to take her to brunch the next morning. They became great friends and spent the rest of the trip together. She later wrote me a note saying, "Because of you, we now have a friend in Croatia who I can't wait to visit next year, and she has an open invitation to Nashville anytime!" It was such a touching story and a reminder that even without the shows, the heart of this community lies in its people, each of us carrying a light that wouldn't exist without one another. Even just writing about it makes me emotional.

Restaurants in Vienna came together to offer free food and do whatever they could to salvage the weekend. Many had already planned Taylor-inspired drinks and meals. Museums even offered free entry—just a quick glance at their Eras Tour ticket, and they were welcomed inside. The city urged fans not to gather in large groups, but that didn't stop us. Every single day of the three shows that were supposed to happen, thousands of fans gathered on Corneliusgasse, a street in Vienna that soon became known as their own *Cornelia Street*. They sang the entire three-and-a-half-hour-long set list, some even performing it with choreography and all. I was home in Nashville, getting chills with every new video that appeared on my feed. Everyone was there! An older couple even opened their apartment windows above the crowded street, set out four speakers, and played Taylor's music for the Swifties below. I had never seen so much strength, unity, and humanity in one place. It's true what they say: Love can conquer all. And we did, in the only way we know how. No evil could take away the one experience in our lives that brings us nothing but pure happiness. They may have robbed us of our shows, but they could never rob us of our joy. Today, a plaque on Corneliusgasse in Vienna stands as a lasting tribute to those nights, honoring the fans who turned heartache into celebration.

The End of an Era

Two years, 149 performed shows, and fifty-one cities later, our Eras Tour journey was finally coming to an end on December 8, 2024. It became the highest-grossing tour of all time, bringing in over $2 billion in ticket sales. I write those statistics because they're relevant, not because they're significant. No number could ever quantify the mark this tour left on our lives—and on Taylor's too.

This tour was two years of friendship bracelets. Two years of companionship. Two years of showing up as your truest self. Two years of pure elation, deep connection, and radical acceptance. Two years of unexpected friendships. Two years of unwavering love. Two years of adventure. Two years of singing your favorite songs alongside the person who wrote them. Two years of livestreams. Two years of dancing like nobody was watching. Two years of looking forward to weekends we'd spend together. All because of one person named Taylor Swift—the force behind it all.

Two years is a long time. When the Eras Tour started, I was working a corporate job where I felt underappreciated and stuck in life. By the time it ended, so much had changed for me.

Along the way, I connected with more of you online than I ever thought possible, started my own business, and made incredible new friends. Most importantly, I found my way again. I think a lot of us did. A fan once commented on my post, saying that she got divorced, remarried, and had a baby within those two years. Another shared that they had gone through two breakups. Even Taylor went through heartbreak and healing, and by the end of the tour had found the kind of love she'd always written about. To some degree, the Eras Tour healed us all, and though we'll miss it dearly, its spirit will live on within us eternally.

One day, these will be the stories we tell our grandchildren. "You got to experience the Eras Tour?" they'll ask. And whether we were there in person or followed along virtually, we'll proudly say yes, before going on to tell them all about it.

Long live our beloved Eras Tour.

CHAPTER NINE

Taylor's Versions

The re-recordings changed everything. They didn't just alter the course of Taylor's career; they reshaped the music industry by redefining music ownership. They also strengthened the bond between Taylor and us in a way none of us could have imagined. What began as a moment of devastation and betrayal, with her masters being sold without her consent, evolved into the most powerful comeback story in music history.

I still remember the day Kelly Clarkson tweeted, "@taylor swift13 just a thought, U should go in & re-record all the songs that U don't own the masters on exactly how U did them but put brand new art & some kind of incentive so fans will no longer buy the old versions. I'd buy all of the new versions just to prove a point." Clearly, Kelly's words resonated, and for every re-recorded album Taylor has released, she's sent Kelly flowers as a thank-you. By reclaiming her work, Taylor didn't just take control of her own narrative—she set a precedent for artists everywhere, proving that creative ownership matters and that there is always a way to fight back.

Despite these albums having existed for years, the re-releases were just as exciting as when they first came out. Each re-recorded album wasn't just about nostalgia; it became a movement. We rallied behind her and celebrated each *Taylor's Version* release as a victory, turning what was once an extremely painful chapter in her life into a triumphant reclamation of her legacy. The new albums gave us new versions of our favorite songs, vault tracks we don't know how we ever lived without, and the rare experience of reliving our past eras with our favorite artist. As if all that wasn't enough, the support we gave her and the success she found through the re-recordings paved the way for what would become one of the biggest moments in both her career and our fandom: the Eras Tour.

Fearless (Taylor's Version)

The day *Fearless (Taylor's Version)* was announced, I felt like I'd stepped into a parallel universe. I couldn't believe we were about to enter the *Fearless* era all over again. I was only eight years old when the original album came out. Far too young to fully appreciate the brilliance of the album rollout. Now it felt different—I got to experience the same songs with a new understanding, as if I were hearing them for the first time.

Just like the old days of capital-letter clues in her CD booklets, Taylor embedded hidden messages in her album announcement, pairing them with golden vault animations and puzzles to decode the six new vault tracks. She made it clear we were officially back in Swiftie-sleuth mode. It seemed like she was inviting us to time travel with her, letting us stand beside her as she reclaimed what should've always been hers. The energy online was indescribable. We were analyzing every clue, decoding every easter egg, and enjoying this new-old era together. Then there was "Mr. Perfectly Fine." The vault song that became an immediate crowd-pleaser. It was the perfect mix of sassy, catchy, and quintessentially bold Taylor. Fans joked about how a certain someone must have woken up that day with his world turned upside down, and the song swiftly earned its place among her greatest breakup anthems.

This era felt golden in every sense. Hearing the re-recorded versions of these songs with her matured voice became a transformative experience. She was no longer the same person who once wrote them, yet it seemed like she was singing them for her younger self, and for all of us who grew up alongside her too. On the new album cover, she faces the opposite direction from the original, no longer fixed on the image of who she was, but instead looking ahead, her hair still flying free. *Fearless (Taylor's Version)* reminded us that while we can't go back in time, we can always revisit who we once were, with new wisdom and strength.

FEARLESS (TAYLOR'S VERSION), featuring six new vault tracks, was released on April 9, 2021.

Red (Taylor's Version)

The *Red* album has always held a special place in our hearts. It's the record that reminds us of the beauty of emotions, that they make life worth living and without them life would lose its color.

Taylor made the greatest mistake ever when she once told a fan that there was a ten-minute version of "All Too Well." Without her letting it slip, and without us pining after it for years on Tumblr, I'm not sure it ever would've seen the light of day. What a shame that would've been, because it's one of the greatest lyrical masterpieces of all time. The *Red (Taylor's Version)* rollout was a personal favorite of mine. It felt so intimate between Taylor and those of us who had been there during the original release. But it was also an era where we welcomed so many new Swifties. My college bar started blasting "All Too Well (10 Minute Version)" every weekend, and I remember the entire place screaming every word. At last, it felt like I wasn't the only die-hard Swiftie in the room. There was always an ongoing joke in the fandom that we wanted to gatekeep Taylor from the general public, who didn't understand her music the way we did. To us, she wasn't a global superstar; she always felt like our indie artist. Well, by this point, the gatekeeping was officially impossible. Millions of new listeners began discovering her unmatched ability to reach people through her lyricism.

Out of all the re-recordings, this one was the longest and most elaborate release. It received critical praise for Taylor's stronger vocals, the polished production, and the nine new vault tracks that turned the album into something even bigger than before. In many ways, it finally got the attention it always deserved. We'd always believed it should have won the Grammy for Album of the Year. For a while, I think Taylor herself felt otherwise, but this release was different. You could tell she poured everything into it, promoting it more than any other *Taylor's Version*, almost as if she was redeeming an album she once critiqued but had now fully embraced as the masterpiece it was. The album cover reflected that transformation too. On the original *Red*, she looked down beneath the brim of a hat, weighed down by heartbreak. On *Red (Taylor's Version)*, she's glowing, eyes lifted toward the horizon, seemingly carrying newfound strength and hope. The timing made it even better: a November release, right in the heart of fall, with leaves on the ground, the air crisp, bringing back memories of Fall 2012.

Taylor once again made this album release feel like something we were all a part of. She held a premiere for *All Too Well: The Short Film* in New York City and invited online Swifties to attend. They sat in a movie theater with Taylor, Dylan O'Brien, and Sadie Sink, all watching it together. When it was over, Taylor picked up a guitar and performed the ten-minute song live for the first time ever. While "All Too Well" was never chosen as a single by the record label, it was chosen by us, and the ten-minute version is the official go-to.

RED (TAYLOR'S VERSION), featuring nine vault tracks, was released on November 12, 2021.

Speak Now (Taylor's Version)

Finally, one of our fan theories actually came true. Taylor had been teasing *Speak Now (Taylor's Version)* quite a bit, especially in her recent "Bejeweled" music video, where she pressed the purple number 3 elevator button. On Friday, May 5, 2023, rumors began swirling that tonight was the night. The John Seigenthaler Pedestrian Bridge outside the Nashville stadium lit up in purple, and true to form, fans were ready to die on the hill that it signaled an announcement. Thankfully, we were right, and this wasn't going down in history as another "five holes in the fence" moment.

This was Taylor's first major announcement on the Eras Tour. It was also my first time seeing the show, and I remember being in complete awe of the performance unfolding right before my eyes. Then, as if it couldn't get any better, she made the announcement. She told us to look at the big screen behind her, and a few seconds later, the new *Speak Now (Taylor's Version)* album cover appeared. Without missing a beat, she launched into "Sparks Fly," grinning as she delivered the lyric "drop everything now." I'm sure we set a new decibel record with how loud all sixty-nine thousand of us shrieked at once . . . And I surely didn't have a voice the next day. Another night we all remember from this album rollout came on June 24, 2023, when Taylor performed "Dear John" as a surprise song and felt the need to remind us to be on our best behavior. "I'm thirty-three years old. I don't care about anything that happened to me when I was nineteen," she said. Of course, the fandom has always been a little overprotective—sometimes holding grudges on her behalf longer than she does—but the fact that she needed to say it made it that much funnier. It was giving *mother*.

On July 7, 2023, the day *Speak Now (Taylor's Version)* was released, Taylor shocked us all by bringing out Taylor Lautner, who cartwheeled and backflipped across the stage. He had allegedly been the inspiration for another revered track, "Back To December," and it was wonderful to see them reunite in such a fun, lighthearted way so many years later. After all, Taylor Lautner and his wife, Tay, are two of the biggest and proudest Swifties out there. Joey King and Presley Cash, who appeared in Taylor's "Mean" music video back in 2010, also joined her onstage to help announce the release of a new music video for "I Can See You," which they also both starred in.

The re-record also sparked conversation about the lyric change in "Better Than Revenge," a shift Swifties understood as a reflection of how times have evolved, while still appreciating the original line for what it was: fiery, teenage, untamed anger. Many of us still admit to singing the original lyric with fond nostalgia.

Out of all the *Taylor's Versions*, the new *Speak Now* cover most closely resembled the original. The facial expression and positioning were nearly identical, but this time, instead of a painting-like image, the cover was a photograph—simpler, yet every bit as enchanting. Like *Fearless (Taylor's Version)*, the direction had been flipped. Both the lyric change and the cover showed how Taylor continues to honor the girl she once was, even as she embraces who she has become.

SPEAK NOW (TAYLOR'S VERSION), featuring six new vault tracks, was released on July 7, 2023.

1989 (Taylor's Version)

On August 9, 2023, the final night of the first US leg of the Eras Tour, *1989 (Taylor's Version)* was announced. From the blue lights flashing as Taylor and *Speak Now* emerged from the vault in the "I Can See You" music video to the symbolic date of 8/9, the easter eggs had been building all along. The timing was simply too perfect, and Swifties could celebrate another victorious summer, having accurately predicted two album announcements in a row.

We had gotten a taste of what the album would sound like when "Wildest Dreams (Taylor's Version)" debuted in 2021 and "This Love (Taylor's Version)" followed in 2022, both featured in movie and TV show trailers. But nothing could have prepared us for the vault tracks. Songs like "Is It Over Now?" and "Say Don't Go" quickly took over our playlists, and rightfully so. For fans who knew all the original album's lore, these tracks added new depth to the album's story, layering in details that made it feel even more complete. At the same time, many of us couldn't help but relate to the heartbreak through them. After all, there's nothing quite like telling someone you love them and them *saying nothing back.*

In 2014, this album reinvented pop music and revolutionized our fandom. It marked Taylor's full crossover into pop, welcoming millions of new fans and cementing her as the biggest artist of our generation. For both us and Taylor, it seemed like nothing could surpass this peak of her influence—radio was ruled by "Style," "Shake It Off," and "Blank Space," while our bedroom walls were covered in Polaroids and photos of New York City. However, nearly a decade later, the Eras Tour proved otherwise, showing that her influence had only soared higher.

With the announcement of *1989 (Taylor's Version)*, we were swept right back into that era: the same songs blasting through our speakers, the same aesthetic revived—only this time with a little more beach and a little less New York. Even the new album cover reflected that change. The original was a Polaroid, cropped to show only the lower half of Taylor's face and a shirt patterned with seagulls, while the re-release featured her smiling in full view against a blue sky where real seagulls flew. It radiated a confidence and freedom that felt like the perfect evolution of the original era.

1989 (TAYLOR'S VERSION), featuring five vault tracks, was released on October 27, 2023, the exact same date as its original release in 2014.

Taylor Swift and *reputation (Taylor's Version)*

As I sit here writing this, I can't help but laugh thinking about how long we spent clowning for a *reputation (Taylor's Version)* announcement. We came up with at least twenty majorly failed fan theories about reputation alone. And *Taylor Swift (Taylor's Version)*? We were convinced it would be the very last re-recording released, symbolically ending with her reclaiming her name through her self-titled debut album. That part, at least, we got right. Though some fans convinced themselves it would be a dramatic double-release event they named "Debutation."

Every date that added up to a number we deemed significant left us spiraling when nothing happened—and sometimes we took it a step too far. At one of the Eras Tour shows, during the surprise song set, a crowd began chanting "*reputation!*" Taylor paused, looked out into the stadium, and said, "Now go sit in a corner and think about what you did," before launching into "Better Than Revenge." It was perfect comedic timing, and honestly, she doesn't get nearly enough credit for how quick-witted she is.

Now, in the greatest plot twist of all time, *reputation (Taylor's Version)* isn't coming. Or at least, not all of it. Because on May 30, 2025, Taylor announced she had done what we never dared believe could happen. She bought back her old masters, winning a fight that had gone on for so much of her career.

She now owned everything she had ever made.

Every album and lyric.

Every music video and concert film.

The album art and photography.

The unreleased songs.

Every single era.

Every part of her story. Of our story.

This moment was grander than any re-recording announcement could have ever been. Because in the end, it was never just about the albums. Yes, we're endlessly grateful for the vault tracks and the new versions of the songs we hold so dear—but fundamentally, it's always been about standing up for her, and standing with her. It was all of us rallying behind her as she reclaimed her life's work, piece by piece, until the puzzle was finally whole again.

"I know, I know. What about Rep TV?" she teased us in her letter. She went on to say that *reputation* is the only album she feels she can't improve. It's fitting, really. In *Miss Americana*, she tearfully said she needed to make a better album after *reputation* wasn't nominated for any of the major Grammy categories. Now, all these years later, she thinks it's perfect—and so do we. A complete arc of growth with the most heartfelt ending. As for the *rep (TV)* vault tracks? She told us that if we want them (and she knows we absolutely do), there will be a time for them to "hatch." If there's one thing we know for sure, it's that they will be "fire," as Taylor once told *Time* magazine. She also reassured us that *Taylor Swift (Taylor's Version)* is fully recorded and she'll release it when the time is right.

Beyond the Re-Recordings

Our steadfast support of Taylor and her decision to re-record and re-release her earlier albums made waves across the music industry. She not only brought heightened awareness to artists' rights to own their work but she also walked a path no major artist had ever taken before. Until Taylor, no prominent musician had re-recorded their entire catalog with the end goal of reclaiming ownership. This was likely because most artists either weren't concerned about owning their masters or didn't have a large enough fan base to make it worth it.

Together, we showed the world two things: that loyalty matters, and that we have the power to influence almost anything. Before this, re-recordings were barely relevant, so most contracts restricted re-recording for only two to three years—which is why she was able to begin releasing hers in 2021. Following the massive success of the *Taylor's Versions*, record labels began changing their contracts with artists, adding clauses preventing them from re-recording their music for up to thirty years.

Outside their impact on the music industry, Taylor's re-recordings solidified her place not only as a cultural icon but also as a savvy businesswoman. She dominated the charts even more than the first time around, while simultaneously captivating a new generation of fans and giving them the chance to grow up with her just as we once did. Through it all, she has kept us at the center of every album release, never losing sight of the personal touches that have made this journey so thrilling and extraordinary since 2006. And yes, as the song goes, *this empire belongs to her.*

13
TS
TS

CHAPTER TEN

Thirteen Life Lessons from Taylor Swift

Life unfolds in unexpected ways, teaching us as we go. The lessons aren't always easy or clear, and sometimes they arrive in the most surprising moments. As we grow, we learn when to let go, when to hold on, when to speak up, and when to listen. While many lessons come from the people closest to us—parents, siblings, or friends—some of the most meaningful wisdom can come from people outside our inner circle. For us, that person has always been Taylor. Aside from her lyrics and memorable quotes, she's taught us countless lessons simply by moving through life with vulnerability, integrity, and unwavering resilience.

Here are my top thirteen:

1. There will never be another like you.

No matter how much success or fame she's achieved, Taylor has always remained true to herself, while encouraging us to do the same. She's shown us that our greatest power lies in our authenticity, and that hiding it would rob the world of our light. It's by sharing that light and stepping fully into who we are that we find our people—the ones who understand us and love us for exactly that, not for who we feel the need to pretend to be.

She has never shied away from evolving publicly, whether it was changing her style, her sound, or her beliefs. Her story reminds us that staying true to ourselves doesn't mean staying the same; it means honoring who we are in each chapter of our lives. At the end of the day, the bravest thing we can be is ourselves.

2. The best revenge is success.

Throughout her life, Taylor has shown us that success is the most powerful form of revenge. When people doubted her or tried to tear her down, she didn't let their words define her or stop her from living out her dream of writing, singing, and performing. Even when giving up might have seemed easier, she transformed that pain into fuel for her art, her growth, and her accomplishments.

Take the *reputation* era, for example. Rather than hiding away, she reclaimed the snake—the very symbol people tried to use against her—and made it her own. As if to say, "You can't control my narrative." One of the *Reputation* Tour's best moments was the opening montage of harsh media commentary, only to be drowned out seconds later by more than sixty thousand fans screaming her lyrics back at her. That is what true victory looks like. Rumor has it she even invited some of those journalists to opening night so they could hear themselves in the montage. If that's true . . . she most definitely is a *savage*.

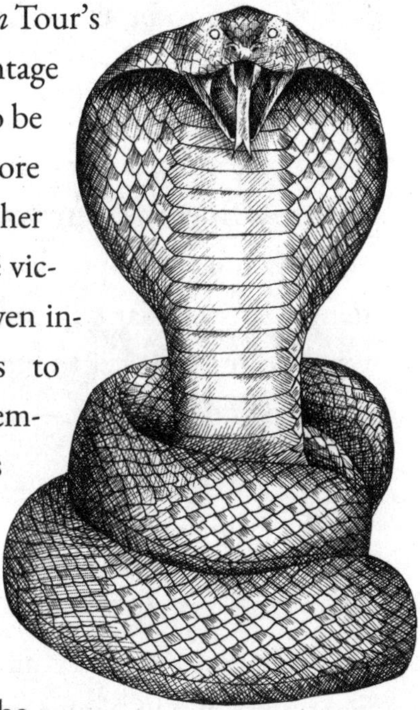

Her approach has never been about hurting those who hurt her. It's always been the "someday I'll be big enough so you can't hit me" kind. It's about rising above, staying focused on what truly matters, and letting karma handle the rest. As she put it best in her 2023 *Time* interview: *"Trash takes itself out every single time."*

3. Know when to stand up for yourself.

Taylor has faced countless challenges that required strength and courage. Perhaps the most significant was when a radio DJ sued her for defamation, blaming her for getting fired after she reported him for sexual harassment. Instead of backing down or settling quietly, she countersued him for just one dollar, a symbolic gesture to show everyone that it was never about the money. It was about standing up for what was right and refusing to be silenced. When she won the case, it wasn't just a victory for her. This was a victory for every woman who has been ridiculed, dismissed, or threatened for speaking up.

It made me prouder than ever to call myself a Swiftie. An office across from the courthouse plastered her lyrics on Post-its in support, and she responded with flowers—a sweet acknowledgment of their solidarity. There was something beautiful about the way we came together to stand behind a woman who empowers others to find their voice—and who lifts up those who might otherwise go unheard.

4. Your energy is expensive.

It's when you lose everything that you discover who your true friends are. When Taylor was no longer the media's American sweetheart, some of the people she thought were her friends disappeared without a trace. Almost as quickly, many of them tried to reappear once she was back on top. It's a reminder to notice who's still there when the spotlight fades. The people who love you in your darkest moments, when you have nothing to offer them but your truest self, are the ones who deserve your time, energy, and above all, your heart. They're the ones who will weather every storm with you. As Taylor once so brilliantly stated, "You should think of your energy as if it's expensive. As if it's like a luxury item. Not everyone can afford it. . . . Not everyone has invested in you in order to be able to have the capital for you to care." Those who have are the ones worth keeping close.

5. Change is a good thing.

One of the greatest career risks Taylor ever took was leaving country music for pop. Everyone told her it would fail and advised her against it, but she trusted her gut. That leap of faith led her to create *1989*, arguably the greatest pop album of all time. Her belief in herself and her work launched her into an entirely new dimension of success, introducing her to millions of new fans. Had she listened to everyone else, she wouldn't be the phenomenon she is today.

Later in her career, she took another risk, this time into folk music, creating two albums that revealed yet another layer of her artistry before eventually returning to the pop genre. Time and time again, she's proved that she is a multidimensional artist. No genre defines her—she redefines the genre. I've always admired the way she has never allowed anyone else to determine her limits or confine her to a single identity. Instead, she continues to reinvent herself in ways that feel authentically her, showing us that change isn't something to fear, but something to embrace. When you trust yourself enough to jump in headfirst, you might just open up a limitless universe of opportunities waiting on the other side.

6. Vulnerability is beautiful.

By sharing her stories with us all these years, Taylor has revealed that there is both beauty and bravery in being open with your emotions and your words. Even though it has sometimes led to harsh headlines and criticism in the media, she has never shied away from being honest in her lyrics. It's in large part what makes her music so relatable, and the reason why our relationship with her feels so personal.

Through her writing, she has demonstrated that vulnerability isn't weakness but strength in its purest form. It takes courage to put your feelings out into the world knowing you might be misunderstood or judged—yet that very risk is what makes genuine connection possible. After all, what would life be if we never formed the bonds that come from revealing our truths? Her willingness to feel it all—love, disappointment, and everything else life has to offer—reminds us to lead our own lives with open hearts, embracing each emotion as it comes. Just remember: *"May your heart remain breakable, but never by the same hand twice."*

7. "Being good to people is a wonderful legacy to leave behind."

Taylor has always lived by these words, consistently extending kindness to fans, friends, and strangers alike. Her care reminds us that goodwill costs nothing but means everything to those who receive it. From giving money to fans she passed on the streets of New York City so they could treat themselves to a nice meal to quietly covering fans' medical bills and tuition during the pandemic to visiting children's hospitals and spending time with the patients, her tenderness has taken many forms.

But her generosity extends well past her fans. She also uses her platform to empower others. Whether she's advocating for artists' rights or supporting fellow musicians by promoting their work to her hundreds of millions of followers, she reminds us that sharing our spotlight with others doesn't diminish our own success—it amplifies it. She has embodied the truth that success and influence should never come at the expense of kindness and compassion. In the words of her grandmother Marjorie: "Never be so clever you forget to be kind, and never wield such power you forget to be polite." Taylor has carried that wisdom forward, gracefully keeping Marjorie's legacy alive.

8. It's okay to be a hopeless romantic.

Life is full of negativity, cynicism, and people who try to suck the joy and innocence out of you as you grow older. They'll say that romance isn't like the books and movies, that your Prince Charming won't appear outside your window with a boom box in hand, ready to sweep you off your feet. They'll call it a fabricated fantasy and suggest you settle for someone nice, even if the spark isn't there. That's exactly why so many of us are drawn to her music. Taylor's songs revive the childlike wonder and romantic imagination we're pressured to bury as adults. She has shown us that it's perfectly okay to dream about grand love stories, handwritten letters, and modern-day fairy tales that begin with something as simple as a friendship bracelet.

She's taught us that it's okay to fall in love more than once, that relationships aren't always perfect, and that heartbreak isn't a sign of failure—it's just proof that you were brave enough to open your heart to someone. And when you do inevitably get hurt, when it feels easier to close yourself off, don't. Closing yourself off only blocks the possibility of true love, the kind that feels magical even on ordinary days, the kind that heals you. So remain open, stay soft, and dare to wear your heart on your sleeve.

9. Be proud of your accomplishments.

Being proud of your accomplishments doesn't make you arrogant; it means you know your worth and recognize your hard work and talent. Too often, women are taught to shrink themselves to avoid making others uncomfortable. Society conditions us to downplay our achievements and never take up too much space—especially in male-dominated industries like entertainment. Taylor has never subscribed to that outdated mindset. *Cue "The Man."*

"The Man" perfectly encapsulates this double standard, highlighting how power and success are praised in men yet criticized in women. She's spoken out about how when men make bold moves, they're seen as strategic, but when women do the exact same thing, they're labeled calculated or manipulative. In this song and throughout her life, she has challenged that narrative. Rather than compete with other women, she uplifts them. When tabloids have tried to pit her against fellow female artists, she has chosen collaboration over competition—inviting them to perform on her tours, publicly cheering on their work, and proving that success multiplies when it's shared. Growing up with her as our role model, we saw her break barriers and own her accomplishments without apology. We learned that confidence in who we are and what we've achieved is not arrogance—it's confidence.

10. Shake it off.

Criticism, jealousy, and negativity are inevitable parts of life, especially when you achieve any form of success. One of the greatest lessons Taylor has taught us is not to let other people's words define our worth. I often think back to her *1989* Tour speeches, when she spoke about choosing which words to let in and which to let go of. Just because someone calls you something doesn't mean you have to accept it as truth. Their words carry weight only if you allow them to. What matters most is staying grounded in your authentic self and refusing to let the noise drown you out. In a society that constantly tries to label us, box us in, and bring us down, she shows us that self-worth is found in *shaking it off*, holding your head high, and continuing to live your life with pride. After all, *haters gonna hate*. Learn to take it as a compliment, because honestly? It's . . . *actually romantic*.

11. You're on your own, kid.

Through these lyrics, she shares a hard truth that many of us must learn firsthand. Life isn't always easy, and sometimes it feels achingly lonely. As she noted in her NYU commencement speech, while it can seem scary to be on your own, it can also be incredibly empowering. Being on your own doesn't just mean having to face challenges by yourself—it means you have the freedom to choose your own path and create your own version of the life you desire. Your own happiness. If you keep pushing through the pain and trust yourself, you'll eventually find what you've been searching for. *Everything you lose is a step you take*, and every ending leads you to your next beautiful beginning.

12. "You'll always find your way back home."

Regardless of how many awards she's won, records she's broken, or stadiums she's sold out, Taylor has always remained rooted in where she came from. She writes about her hometown, her family, her childhood bedroom, her best friend Abigail, and her first heartbreaks with the same authenticity she brings to her most recent work. Back in her 2004 *Good Morning America* interview in Nashville, she spoke about her biggest dream—not about fame but about inspiring young girls the way LeAnn Rimes had inspired her, reaching people through music without even knowing them.

After she reclaimed ownership of her masters, it felt only right that the first place she performed was her adopted hometown of Nashville. Returning there after gaining full control of her life's work wasn't just significant—it was the ultimate homecoming, demonstrating that no matter how far you go, staying anchored in your beginnings keeps you grounded in who you truly are. No matter how much you grow or how many dreams you make come true, always honor the version of yourself who once wished for all you have now.

13. Love yourself in every era.

Taylor's entire career is proof of what it means to fully embrace every version of yourself. She's been the country sweetheart, the fearless teenager, the heartbroken girl wearing outfits she once described as "1950s housewife," the pop sensation dominating the global stage, and the woodland fairy writing quietly from her cabin in the woods. Each phase of life molded her into the person she is today.

She teaches us that all of our eras matter. That loving yourself isn't just about who you are right now—it's about loving the person you were too. The version of you who didn't know as much, who made mistakes, who tried things that now make you cringe. After all, that just means you were daring enough to take the steps that led you here. So instead of looking back in embarrassment at your old photos, your questionable fashion choices, your dramatic journal entries, or the people you once loved, just be grateful for every past version of yourself. They're not something to erase or hide from; they're proof of your growth, your resilience, and your ever-evolving story.

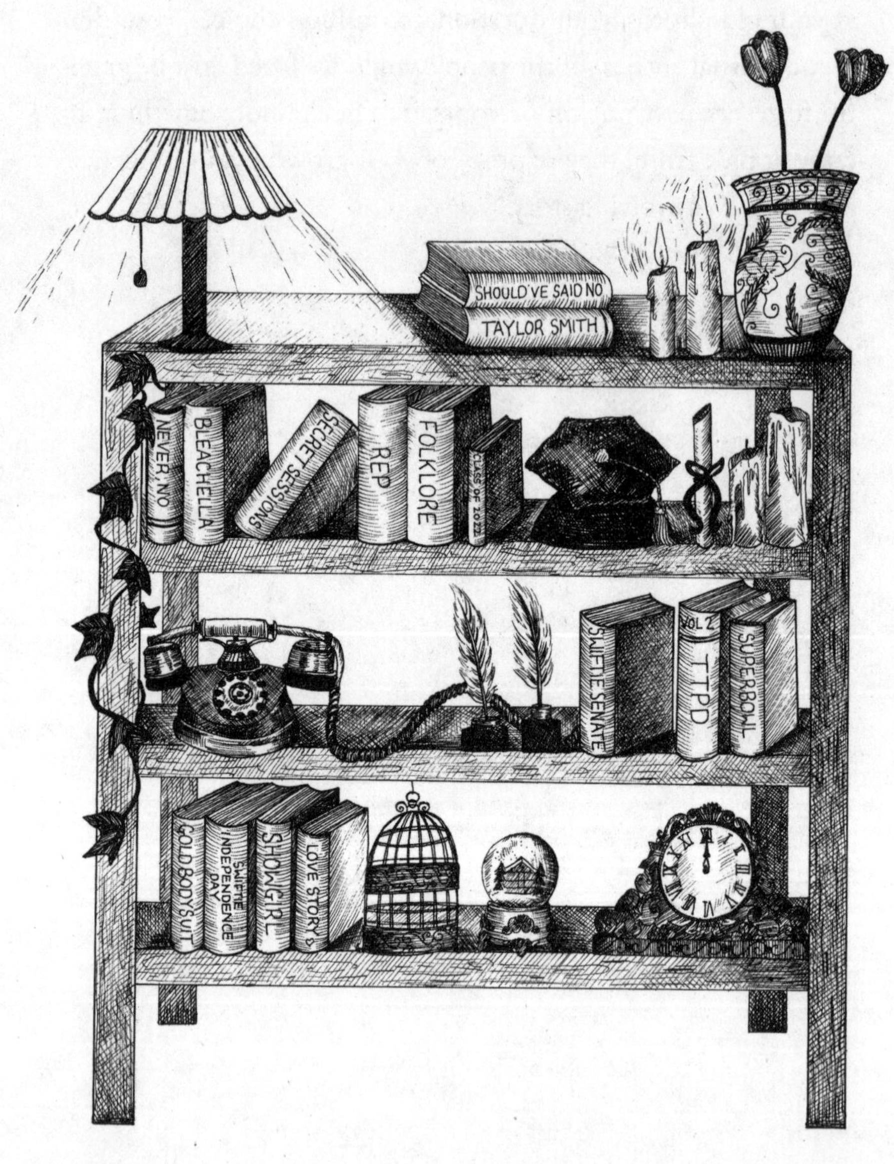
SHOULD'VE SAID NO
TAYLOR SMITH
NEVER, NO
BLEACHELLA
SECRET SESSIONS
REP
FOLKLORE
CLASS OF 2022
SWIFTIE SENATE
VOL 2
TTPD
SUPERBOWL
GOLD BODYSUIT
SWIFTIE INDEPENDENCE DAY
SHOWGIRL
LOVE STORY

CHAPTER ELEVEN

Fifteen Historic Days in Swiftie History

There are certain days that live on in Swiftie history—days that might seem ordinary to everyone else but hold a deep meaning for us. Some are dates we mark on our calendars, others are ones we can recall down to where we were when they happened, and a few are so legendary we'll still be talking about them fifty years from now. Whether they brought on laughter, cheers, tears, or chaos, these moments have become part of a story that only we understand, and that's what makes them *ours*.

There are infinite historic Swiftie days, but here are my top *fifteen*.

1. Taylor's Performance of "Should've Said No" at the CMA Awards

MAY 18, 2008

This remains one of Taylor's most defining performances. For many, it was the one that put her on the map, revealing the dynamic performer she was destined to become. She began by sitting on a chair wearing a black hoodie and sweatpants, the perfect embodiment of teenage angst. As she approached the first chorus, two dancers ripped off her hoodie and sweats to reveal a black-and-silver sparkly dress underneath. Oh, the drama.

By the third chorus, she was belting in a higher key while rain poured down on her from above. This wasn't a typical performance for the CMA Awards, especially at a time when country music was still such a heavily male-led genre. Whether you were in the arena or watching from home, you could feel the weight of her stage presence. As always, she wore her emotions on her sleeve, making every person watching feel the longing, desperation, betrayal, and raw honesty in her every word. This performance cemented her as not just a country singer but a performer in every sense of the word.

2. That *Vogue* Photoshoot

JANUARY 24, 2012

Ahead of the *Red* era, she officially debuted full blunt bangs for her *Vogue* cover shoot—a style that instantly became symbolic and signaled the grown-up, more daring Taylor we'd see in the years to come. She hasn't ditched the bangs since.

Of course, this wasn't the last time Taylor used her hair to make a statement. Fast-forward to the final night of the European leg of the *Red* Tour, when she stunned everyone by chopping her signature long curls into a sleek shoulder-length bob. She shared a backstage video of the cut, surrounded by her friends, band, and team members cheering her on. To all of us, including Taylor, it wasn't just any haircut—it marked the end of one era and the birth of another. It was a reinvention in real time. With a chop like that, it was clear she was ready to leave country behind and step fully into her pop-star era. Polaroids, synth-pop anthems, and crop tops were on the horizon.

Then in April 2016, she posted a cryptic selfie flaunting her newly bleached hair with the caption "BLEACHELLA." While it seemed like just a Coachella moment, it turned out to be the start of an edgier aesthetic—a precursor to the *reputation* era. Maybe not quite as shocking as the *1989* chop, but still a shift that sent us into collective mania. With Taylor, every style change carries significance.

3. "Taylor Smith, Everyone"

APRIL 1, 2012

The "Taylor Smith" moment remains one of the most treasured inside jokes in our fandom. It happened at the 2012 Academy of Country Music Awards when a red-carpet reporter interviewed Taylor, ending the conversation by turning to the camera and saying, "Taylor Smith, everyone." Taylor instantly started giggling and looked around to see if anyone else heard it. For a second, it looked like she considered correcting the woman, but then she just let it slide, smiling politely. Of course, we took this moment and ran with it, turning "Taylor Smith" into a long-running meme we still reference to this day.

4. Taylor at the Billboard Music Awards

MAY 19, 2013

If you search this day on social media, you'll find endless montages of clips that have become firmly embedded in Swiftie culture. We often say Taylor "chose violence" that night, but in reality, she just wasn't in the mood for the over-the-top award show theatrics and ridiculous questions. Who could blame her?

From the second she stepped onto the red carpet, it was clear she wasn't playing games. A reporter asked, "Have you ever regretted writing a song about one of your exes?" Without missing a beat, she confidently replied, "Never . . . No, because you don't write a song about them unless you know that you don't really wanna know them anymore." Another reporter asked an unprofessional, headline-baiting question, and she immediately shut it down with "Can we have another question?" Then, when someone babbled about lip-syncing, she cut him off: "Well, I didn't, so."

It was a night of unbothered and unfiltered Taylor, and we enjoyed every second of it. But what truly took the cake? When she took the media's jokes about her dating life and turned it into a dedication to us: "To the fans who come to the shows, who buy the albums, I just want you to know this one thing: You are the longest and best relationship I have ever had," making it clear to everyone that she was there not for the industry politics, but for us.

5. The Very First *1989* Secret Session

SEPTEMBER 20, 2014

This was the day Taylor hosted the first Secret Session at her Los Angeles home. Fans began posting online that they had just left Taylor's house, but still, many of us questioned whether it was real. As more and more confirmed it, the news spread across Tumblr, eventually making national headlines the next day.

She went on to host Secret Sessions at her four other homes in New York, Nashville, Rhode Island, and London. No one could believe that she had actually invited fans to hang out, bake cookies, listen to unreleased songs, and talk like old friends. Following every Secret Session, if someone went silent on their fan account for even a day, the rest of us would instantly wonder if they'd been invited. More often than not, we were right.

Those experiences made us believe that maybe, just maybe, we too could meet Taylor one day and express our appreciation in person. To outsiders, it seemed unimaginable that a global pop star would invite her most devoted fans—the ones who ran entire social media pages dedicated to her—into her own home. Yet that's exactly what she did, to show her gratitude for our relentless dedication that fueled her art. Those gestures bonded us as a community, both in person and online.

Though she hasn't hosted Secret Sessions since 2017, Taylor still finds ways to create that same intimate experience. The *Life of a Showgirl* theater release brought fans together to celebrate her music and explore the meaning behind the songs, creating a gathering much like a Secret Session. Classic Taylor: always coming up with innovative ways to bring us closer.

6. The Social Media Blackout

AUGUST 18, 2017

I will never forget where I was on this day. It was a jaw-dropping event in *the life of a Swiftie*. For about a year after snake-gate, Taylor had completely disappeared. She was absent on social media, leaving us with nothing but speculation. #TS6, representing Taylor's sixth album, had been trending on Twitter and Tumblr all year, but for the first time in a long time, it felt like we genuinely had no clue what her next move was.

Then, on August 18, Taylor wiped her social media pages clean, turned her website dark, and unfollowed every account across platforms, with the sole exception of the Swifties on Tumblr. We were floored. What in the world was happening? What was she planning? If you were in the fandom then, think back to what you were doing when it happened—I bet you know exactly where you were.

Three days later, she broke her silence with three cryptic videos that, when viewed together, formed a slithering snake. It was chilling—I still get goose bumps thinking about it. On August 23, she officially announced the *reputation* album and revealed its cover art, which resembled a newspaper collage full of headlines. Right then, we knew this was her direct response to the media, who had eagerly jumped on the hate train the very first chance they got. They tried to destroy her reputation, but Taylor came back stronger than ever, owning the villain narrative they created for her and turning it into a killer success. "The old Taylor can't come to the phone right now. Why? Oh, 'cause she's dead!" became everyone's new favorite lyric overnight. Like a snake shedding its skin, she emerged renewed: stronger, wiser, and totally badass. It was the ultimate comeback, and we were all *ready for it*.

7. *Folklore* Album Release

JULY 24, 2020

Speaking of album releases, *folklore* was one for the history books. Dropping it out of nowhere was already a seismic event, but it came at a time when we needed it most—in the middle of a global pandemic, when so many of us felt anxious and disconnected from the rest of humanity. This album felt like a warm, melancholic hug. It gave us something to hold on to and secret gardens to escape into when reality felt unbearably heavy.

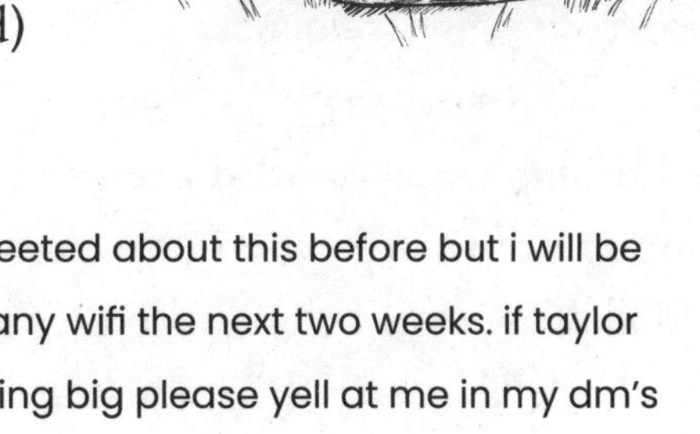

Not only did *folklore* save us in more ways than one but it also created one of the most viral storylines in Swiftie Twitter history. On July 18, 2020, a fan named Delphine (username @seeitinmymind) tweeted:

> oomfs, i've already tweeted about this before but i will be without my phone or any wifi the next two weeks. if taylor decides to do something big please yell at me in my dm's and don't unfollow me for inactivity xxx

Sure enough, on July 24, Taylor surprise-released *folklore* while Delphine was away on a camping trip. When she finally returned to Twitter, she had to catch up on everything she had missed, posting her live reactions to the album, and to Taylor herself, who replied to her tweet:

> Welcome back from your trip! We are all somber woodland fairies now. Feel free to grab a wicker basket and join us.

A response that perfectly encapsulated the enchantment of this era—an unexpected universe we all stepped into together, barefoot in our imaginary woodsy cabins, wrapped in moss and cardigans, feeling just a little less isolated.

8. Dr. Taylor Swift

MAY 18, 2022

On this day, Taylor received an honorary doctor of fine arts degree from New York University. While many people at age eighteen are heading off to college, she had been writing albums, touring the world, and winning Grammys. Still, academia wanted to formally recognize the cultural impact she had made through her art, storytelling, and influence.

With the rest of the NYU class of 2022 in attendance, she walked triumphantly across the renowned Yankee Stadium field in her purple cap and gown to accept her degree—with her bodyguard following close behind, also dressed in a cap and gown to seamlessly blend in with the graduates. Then came a particularly memorable speech, where she shared the life lessons she had learned by age thirty-two. She spoke candidly about her successes, failures, and growth, offering heartfelt wisdom to a stadium full of graduates as they prepared to enter a brand-new chapter of their lives.

Seemingly teaching everyone how to pause and ground themselves, she said, "We will breathe in, breathe through, breathe deep, and breathe out." At the time, we didn't realize these words were also lyrics to "Labyrinth," a song on her upcoming *Midnights* album. Of course, it wouldn't be a Taylor speech without an easter egg hidden in plain sight. Moments like these reveal why she feels like both a friend and a mentor—someone who can turn even a commencement speech into something that feels like a comforting therapy session and a piece of poetry all at once.

9. Swifties in the Senate

JANUARY 23, 2023

Following the disastrous Eras Tour presale in November 2022, concert ticket scalping had become a national conversation. The presale had caused Ticketmaster's platform to crash, leaving millions of us devastated and without tickets. To make matters worse, the highly anticipated general public on-sale was canceled altogether due to a lack of remaining seats.

Fast-forward two months, and Swifties were suddenly being referenced in the US Senate Judiciary Committee hearing on January 23, 2023. Lawmakers acknowledged that we were a powerful force in exposing the flaws of Ticketmaster's practices. Never in a million years did we think senators would sit there quoting Taylor Swift lyrics, but that day, they did just that. Senator Richard Blumenthal referenced "Anti-Hero," saying, "Ticketmaster ought to look in the mirror and say, 'I'm the problem, it's me.'" Meanwhile, Senator Amy Klobuchar nodded to another track, stating, "You can't have too much consolidation—something that, unfortunately for this country, as an ode to Taylor Swift, I will say, we know 'All Too Well.'"

It felt like Ticketmaster and Live Nation were finally being held accountable. Years later, the conversation is still ongoing. Once again, we showed everyone just how influential we are as a community.

10. Super Bowl LVIII

FEBRUARY 11, 2024

Taylor had her final Tokyo show in Japan, the night before attending her first Super Bowl, and we were all anxiously wondering whether she would make it back to Las Vegas in time for kickoff. Fans, sports analysts, and news outlets alike were busy calculating time zones and private jet flight durations, trying to figure out if it was even humanly possible. It got to the point that the Japanese embassy in Washington, DC, decided to chime in, releasing an official statement addressing the situation.

It read:

> *The Embassy of Japan in the United States is aware of recent media reports concerning the steps Taylor Swift will need to take to travel from Tokyo after her concert on February 10th to Las Vegas in time to watch the Kansas City Chiefs play in Super Bowl LVIII. Despite the 12-hour flight and 17-hour*

time difference, the Embassy can confidently Speak Now to say that if she departs Tokyo in the evening after her concert, she should comfortably arrive in Las Vegas before the Super Bowl begins. We know that many people in Japan are excited to experience Taylor Swift's Eras Tour, so we wanted to confirm that anyone concerned can be Fearless in knowing that this talented performer can wow Japanese audiences and still make it to Las Vegas to support the Chiefs when they take the field for the Super Bowl wearing Red.

It seemed as though the entire world was collectively rooting for the perfect moment in a love story that had been unfolding before our eyes. Taylor used her Tayvoodoo manifesting powers to win the Super Bowl (by association) in her very first NFL season. From watching her cheer at Sunday games to that scene straight out of a movie when she went down to the field after the win and said, "Jet lag is a choice," it was definitely one of those *you-just-had-to-be-there days.*

11. *TTPD* Double-Album Release

APRIL 19, 2024

We had been dreaming about (and incorrectly predicting) double albums for quite some time. While we're often way off target when it comes to what Taylor's announcements will be, we do occasionally get the timing right. Keyword being "occasionally."

Take the 2024 Grammys, for example. She showed up wearing black and white, so of course, we were bracing ourselves for *reputation (Taylor's Version)*. But instead, she did what she always does best: the unthinkable. While accepting her award for Best Pop Vocal Album for *Midnights*, she casually dropped the bombshell that she would be releasing a new album, *The Tortured Poets Department*. The rest of the world was focused on the album reveal itself, yet we were busy fixating on something else entirely. *Why did she hold up two fingers?* It felt far too deliberate and random to be insignificant.

Three days before the album release, we noticed a few easter eggs at the Los Angeles album pop-up event—some of which, of course, only reinforced our belief that a double album was coming. There was a peace sign hand statue, which we interpreted as a subtle nod to "two," just like the peace sign Taylor held up at the Grammys. We also noticed a clock set to two o'clock, another clearly intentional reference.

Perhaps the most intriguing clue came from the album's hidden message on Apple Music, which read: "We hereby conduct this post mortem." "Postmortem" refers to an examination after death, which led us to think about rigor mortis, a process that begins approximately *two* hours after death. One thing about Swifties is that we are relentless detectives, sometimes connecting dots that may or may not exist. There's nothing more thrilling than seeing our most far-fetched theories come to fruition.

Finally, April 19 arrived, and when the clock struck midnight, it was time. Some of us gathered at listening parties; others sat alone in our rooms with headphones on, myself included, knowing that our lives would never be the same once we hit play. We listened in order, because that's the way Taylor Swift albums are meant to be experienced—each song a page in this chapter of her story. By 1:30 a.m., we were already on our second listen. Some

Swifties dove straight into lyric dissections, others shared their reactions online, while many of us just kept scrolling, eager to see if our thoughts and feelings lined up with the rest of the fandom. Just as we were fully immersed in the new album, it happened: She dropped a second one. Suddenly fifteen more songs were ours—a double album titled *The Anthology*.

This day was historic for myriad reasons. Mainly, because we had accurately predicted the double album, a theory we'd held on to with equal parts hope and healthy clownery. But also because this album arrived exquisitely raw and emotionally complex—the kind only Taylor can deliver.

12. The Gold Bodysuit Debut

OCTOBER 18, 2024

We spent the entirety of the Eras Tour clowning for *reputation (Taylor's Version)*. Throughout the tour, Taylor had debuted new outfits for every era except for *reputation*—her same red-and-black snake bodysuit making an appearance night after night. After her post-international break, we were all convinced that Miami would be the city where she'd finally announce the album. Why? Because at *The Tortured Poets Department* album release event in Los Angeles, there was a globe with a pin stuck in Miami. Reading that back now, I realize just how far gone we were.

I was at the first Miami show when Taylor stepped onto the stage wearing a new gold-and-black *reputation* bodysuit, and in my twenty-four years of life, I had never felt an energy shift like that before. The stadium exploded with screams and gasps, everyone thinking this was it: The moment had finally arrived. I've always loved how we all instantly latch onto the same little details.

One of Taylor's greatest talents is her ability to build anticipation while keeping her next move completely unpredictable. There was no announcement that night, but it was still noteworthy. We're no strangers to being wrong when it comes to decoding easter eggs. Sometimes I even wonder if we've dreamed up theories Taylor herself never thought of—only for her to run with them because they made too much sense.

13. Swiftie Independence Day

MAY 30, 2025

None of us ever imagined this day would come. For years, we streamed *Taylor's Version*s, rallied behind her vault tracks, and supported her reclaiming her life's work. But what happened on May 30, 2025, felt like something even our wildest fan theories couldn't have predicted: Taylor Swift announced that she had bought back her masters. She now owned everything she had ever created.

We immediately took to streaming platforms to celebrate in the most Swiftie way possible: by making history. Within hours, the *reputation* album ranked at number one and the Taylor Swift album ranked at number two on the US iTunes chart. Even more groundbreaking, Taylor became the first artist ever to have her entire catalog, both the original and re-recorded versions, simultaneously chart within the US iTunes Top 100.

To some, it may have looked like nothing more than another chart takeover. To us, it meant that when millions stand beside someone fighting for justice, *the walls that they put up to hold us back will fall down, but we'll stand up champions.*

Swiftie Independence marks the day Taylor finally reclaimed everything she worked so hard for—and we got to be part of making it happen. She gave us songs that healed us, and by showing up at the Eras Tour, we gave her everything she needed to reclaim them.

14. *The Life of a Showgirl* Announcement

AUGUST 12, 2025

The lead-up began the day before, when the *New Heights* podcast posted a cryptic silhouetted image that looked suspiciously like Taylor. We noticed immediately but hesitated to let ourselves believe it. Then came the countdown on her website. Suddenly, we knew something real was happening. At 12:12 a.m. on August 12, the new album appeared on her site, and a clip went live on her account confirming it: Taylor herself, announcing *The Life of a Showgirl* on *New Heights.* Within minutes, social media turned orange—every brand with a savvy strategist was promoting their product against an orange backdrop. It was official. The color orange now belonged to Taylor Swift too.

The very next day, August 13, she officially made her podcasting debut. Productivity plummeted as Swifties everywhere admitted they couldn't focus on work—deadlines ignored, meetings skipped, and more than a few fans calling out altogether just to stream it in peace. Some of us even went as far as changing our flights. Wherever we were, we tuned in to the full two-hour episode and hung on every word. We got a glimpse of her newfound obsession with sourdough, tried to decode the easter eggs we knew she'd tucked into the background and her phrasing, and kept track of the numbers she casually dropped, ones we knew must have held significance even if we couldn't yet understand their meaning.

Taylor had gone years without doing much public-facing press, but this felt bigger than any TV or talk show she'd ever done. Instead of awkward, invasive questions, we got her on her own terms, sharing her life with us. This wasn't an interview. It felt like a FaceTime with friends. She opened up about the album's story and revealed she'd been writing it during the Eras Tour, flying back and forth to Sweden on her rare days off. Our favorite part of it all? We saw her so adored, so confident, and so at ease on camera, which filled us with sheer parasocial joy. Absolutely none of us were mentally prepared for what was coming next.

15. Today Was a Fairy Tale

AUGUST 26, 2025

Your English teacher and your gym teacher are getting married.

Taylor posted her engagement photos, officially announcing the news, and within seconds our feeds morphed. It felt like a royal engagement, because to us, that's exactly what it was. At the center of it all was the ring itself—an old mine brilliant-cut diamond with fifty-eight handcrafted facets, the two digits, of course, adding up to Taylor's lucky number, thirteen. With its cushion-like shape, glowing yellow-gold setting, and antique charm, it felt intrinsically "Taylor Swift." Timeless and elegant, it was a rare piece carefully co-designed by her future husband.

Breaking headlines ran across every major network, and timelines filled with nothing but awe, congratulations, and pure celebration. Even companies joined in, posting products with rings around them and offering 13 percent off "Tayvis" discounts. Restaurant chains volunteered to cater the wedding, and Swifties offered to clean the toilets at the venue. Panera Bread posted a loaf of bread stamped with the words "SHE SAID YEAST!", while jewelers scrambled to replicate the one-of-a-kind diamond ring. It was utter pandemonium.

It was contagious—everyone reacted as if they themselves had gotten engaged. Our phones buzzed with messages from people we hadn't heard from in years, congratulating us simply

because they knew how thrilled we'd be about the news. Swifties were being called up for live interviews on Fox and CNN; my segment aired from a cruise ship somewhere in the middle of the ocean.

Yet, looking back, none of it was really a surprise. Just thirteen days earlier on the podcast, the depth of their care for one another was clear. We'd never seen anyone be so openly supportive of her. He lit up when she shone, and she did the same for him. Eighty-seven and thirteen—together they *kept it one hundred*, perfectly completing each other.

The announcement felt like a dream realized. For the girl we grew up with, who endured so much hardship and judgment, who spent two decades writing songs of yearning and heartbreak, and who never stopped hoping—this was the happily-ever-after we had always wished for her. For those of us still waiting to find it, it offers a faith worth holding on to. As the news rippled through the community, Swifties began sharing how her story gave them the courage to rewrite their own. Post after post flooded social media from fans saying they had recently walked away from relationships, or refused to settle, because Taylor demonstrated what it means not to compromise on what they truly deserve. As comedian Nikki Glaser joked, their bond might just "ruin some relationships" by showing us what's possible.

Above all, we were grateful she chose to share the engagement with us. She knows we've been on this journey alongside her from the very beginning, and her letting us into this milestone meant everything. Thanks to Ed Kelce—the Swifties' new honorary dad—we soon discovered that the proposal had happened right after the podcast's taping, with Travis hiring florists to build her very own garden in their backyard. In "I Hate It Here," she sings about secret gardens in her mind—the places she goes to when life feels too heavy. He took that fantasy and made it a reality, turning her imagination into something she could walk into, so she no longer had to escape. Her safe place was now with him.

US

CHAPTER TWELVE

The Stories of Us

There's something about this fandom that feels permanent. Maybe it's the way we show up for each other, the language we share, or how Taylor's music has seamlessly embedded itself into our everyday lives. Even when the records stop spinning and the tours eventually come to an end, we aren't going anywhere. The friendships we've formed, the memories we carry, and the ways this community has shaped who we are feel eternal, and being part of it has never been just about Taylor or any one person—it's always been about all of us. To honor that, I turned to the voices of Swifties themselves, inviting fans through my platform to share their personal stories.

What follows is a collection of reflections that show just how deeply this experience has touched our lives. The words come from different voices and corners of the world, yet they're all bound by the same *thread of gold*. My hope is that they capture the magic we've created and remind us how lucky we are to have all experienced it together.

When You Think Happiness

Our fandom has become a lifeline, a place to lean on one another in the hardest of times. And although Taylor's music is what drew us in, this community is a large part of the reason so many of us are still here today. For some, it has meant finally finding what we had been searching for, whether that was empathy, support, or connection. In a society that often praises the appearance of perfection, we gave each other permission to find strength in our imperfections. The friendships we've formed run deep—some started online or at concerts, while others unfolded by complete happenstance. However they began, the result is the same: a spark of recognition, the remarkable feeling of finding someone who sees the world the way you do. When asked how being in this fandom has changed your lives, here's what some of you shared:

It helped me believe in the power of girlhood again. The joy, camaraderie, and creativity we've always been willing to share. It helped me find a part of myself I was severely missing.

All of my current close friends are Swifties. I may not have met them all because of the fandom, but it brought us closer. We attend Taylor-themed parties and concerts and love traveling together. I honestly don't know what my life would look like without them.

I was heavily bullied for four years and ended up suffering from an eating disorder and severe anxiety. Being in the Swiftie community gave me an outlet to connect with people around the world who love Taylor and her music like I do. I'm forever grateful.

It's made me feel more confident in embracing my femininity and outspokenness.

I met one of my closest friends in Walmart thanks to my Eras Tour T-shirt! The community has brought me more joy, hope, love, and happiness than I ever thought possible, and I never want that feeling to fade. I've made friends from every corner of the world, and I've shared things with them that my own family doesn't know, all because Taylor's music has helped me heal my inner child and overcome depression and anxiety.

It made me feel like I belong to a family. Like I'm part of something big. We've made our own joyful planet, and we just get each other.

When the Vienna shows got canceled, we all still celebrated together. It reminded me this goes beyond music—it's about connection.

I always wear two friendship bracelets everywhere I go, just in case I meet a fellow Swiftie. I've done this so many times, and it's led me to so many beautiful conversations and connections. Being a Swiftie gave me the best community I could imagine.

Once I find out someone's a Swiftie, it's like an instant connection.

Eight or Nine to Eighty-Nine

Taylor's music is for everyone.

I once saw a video of an older woman hearing "The Smallest Man Who Ever Lived" for the first time. Initially she sat and listened quietly. But as the song unfolded, something shifted—her eyes welled with tears, her face softened with recognition, and you could almost sense the lyrics touching something buried: an old pain, a betrayal, a distant memory she thought she'd forgotten. Even if the heartbreak happened years ago, Taylor's words unearthed feelings that had never truly healed and offered comfort. At the end, the woman simply asked to hear the song again. That impulse is the best way I can describe Taylor's music. It's not just the music we listen to; it's the music we return to. Her songs become our companions through pain, tools for processing, and, ultimately, places of refuge. There's peace in feeling heard, and there's something profoundly human about choosing to sit with a song that hurts—because it lets you know that you're going to be okay.

No matter our age, her lyrics have a way of peeling back the layers of our emotions and reminding us that our feelings are not only valid but worthy of being voiced.

Your stories that follow illustrate how her songs have resonated across every generation and every walk of life, because they speak to the universal human experience.

I was in fourth grade when my mom called me into the garage early before school. My dad hadn't left yet and was filming—strange. She told me she'd won tickets to the 1989 Tour off the radio. I screamed, cried, and wore a blue sparkly dress to the show. We've gone to every Taylor tour together since. I even got to return the favor and surprise her with Eras Tour tickets. She definitely lost some of her hearing from when Taylor came out in the new gold reputation bodysuit that night.

I gave my daughter the Debut CD in her Easter basket when she was six. Now she's getting married. For the past fifteen years, Taylor's music has been the soundtrack of our relationship. We've danced, laughed, cried, and grown up together.

I grew up a Swiftie, and now I'm a mother. My daughter and I didn't get Eras Tour tickets, so we drove from Oklahoma to Indianapolis just to try.

The tickets didn't work out, but we had three days of alone time—just us, singing Taylor's songs. I wouldn't trade that for anything.

I've been a Swiftie since I was a kid, but now the best part is having my seven-year-old daughter sing and dance with me to Taylor every day. There's no better feeling.

During Covid, it was obviously a strange and isolating time. My daughters and I bonded to an even stronger level as we listened to folklore and evermore every day. Those albums connected us with the Swiftie world, and we didn't feel as alone anymore.

I've been a Swiftie since 2006—since I was seven! My dad, a huge country fan, brought home her album thinking I'd like it. Since then, we've been to almost every tour together. Taylor opened him up to other music, and her concerts have become our tradition. No other fandom feels as pure, joyful, or safe.

When I was four, my mom would blast Red in the car and around the house. Her favorite song was "All Too Well." I learned every song just for her. Over the years, I became a huge Swiftie too. Her favorite album is

still Red, mine is folklore. I couldn't get her Eras tickets, but we went to the film and sang our hearts out. I've never felt so close to her.

My daughter and I have always been close, but being Swifties together brought us even closer. We flew to Vancouver for the final show and had the most amazing time.

My seven-year-old daughter became a Swiftie during the pandemic, watching me jam out to Taylor on repeat. She desperately wanted to go to the Eras Tour. I couldn't get tickets, but my husband surprised us with Toronto tickets for my fortieth. Watching my daughter watch Taylor was a core memory I'll never forget.

My tween daughter and I sometimes struggle to connect, but our love for Taylor grounds us. Her music helps us reset, dance, and come back together.

I was at Nashville Night 1 with my mom when Taylor announced Speak Now (Taylor's Version). That album was my favorite as a kid, and to experience it live with my mom again was so special.

Dancing with my two sons to "Lover" in the kitchen after waiting two years to see the Eras Tour—finally making it to Night 3 in New Orleans—was pure magic. A moment I'll never forget.

You're *Not* On Your Own, Kid

Whether it's sharing theories or helping others make it to a show, this community has been a steady presence in our lives. I invited some of you to share what it has meant to you, and these are just a few of your answers that moved me. Your words are why I started my fan account, and why I can't imagine ever walking away.

When I joined the fandom online in 2011, I was struck by the kindness in the Swiftie community. As I struggled to adjust to university and felt out of place, this space made me feel seen—even as a silent observer. I couldn't afford concerts, but reading others' experiences, especially during reputation, reminded me that connection and compassion still exist.

I've always loved Taylor's music—my first concerts were the Red and 1989 Tours. I missed the Reputation Tour because I had just had my son, and during that time I was battling postpartum depression, grieving my mom's death, and supporting my sister through cancer. Taylor's music

became a lifeline, offering moments of escape and healing. It wasn't until the Eras Tour that I found a community of fans who understood just how deeply her lyrics can soothe even the wounds we didn't know we had.

I made a wonderful friend who also follows you. She's from Brazil, and I live in Texas. We talk every day now. It has absolutely felt like a community, following you and seeing all the camaraderie; it's exceptional!

Found my Amsterdam Eras Tour tickets through a fellow Swiftie and met another very nice Swiftie from Germany who took me to the concert. I felt so blessed.

Being a Swiftie is incredible. Everyone is so loving, so caring, so supportive of each other, and so accepting. The community wouldn't be the same without each and every one of us!

I got Miami Night 1 tickets through you on Instagram, and being able to go with my friend Carly—especially after missing out on Vienna—meant everything. Experiencing the gold rep bodysuit live for the first time was a core memory. That night brought us even closer, and I'm so grateful we got to experience it together.

At the Zurich show, I saw a girl crying as "All Too Well" started. She was alone and had no friendship bracelets, so I gave her my "All Too Well" bracelet. We stood side by side, crying and laughing. It was a moment of connection I'll never forget.

I went to the Eras Tour in Paris Night 4 alone, and my anxiety was eating me alive—until a woman approached me out of nowhere and said, "You're here on your own? Me too." We ended up singing our hearts out, dancing, laughing, and having the best night of our lives. We exchanged Instagrams—she's from Australia, I'm from Tunisia—and somehow, we found each other in that magical crowd.

Being a Swiftie has given me a safe, understanding community that truly "gets" why Taylor's songs mean so much. When I was going through chemo, two moms of fellow Swifties—people I barely knew—sent me Taylor merch because they saw I wore it to every appointment. Their kindness meant the world.

I'll never forget my first time seeing Taylor on the Speak Now tour, and then singing with thousands of Swifties in the streets of Vienna during

Eras when the concert was canceled. Even in those unexpected moments, strangers were stopping me in the streets to exchange friendship bracelets.

I got my first-ever Taylor concert ticket on my birthday—and it turned out to be the best experience of my life. I'll never forget how that night made me feel, or the people who helped make it happen.

Hold on to the Memories

Taylor's music has accompanied us through a lifetime of experiences—first dances at weddings, cross-country road trips, quiet nights alone, and loud ones spent screaming lyrics in packed stadiums. "Love Story" played during a proposal. "You Belong With Me" blasted through a childhood bedroom during a sleepover. Some walked across graduation stages with "Long Live" echoing in their minds, while others rocked newborn babies to sleep to the gentle lull of "Never Grow Up." We've danced in the kitchen with our parents to "Shake It Off" and collapsed on our bedroom floors crying to "Bigger Than The Whole Sky," grieving a love—or a life—we'd hoped would go on forever. Her songs are present in every chapter of life: the highs, the lows, and all the shades that lie between.

Your quotes below offer a glimpse into the ways she has been there for us through life's most pivotal moments.

I grew up with Taylor Swift's music thanks to my Aunt Carrie, who was my best friend. We'd sing together in the car, especially to Speak

Now. She passed away in the 2011 Alabama tornado outbreak, and ever since, Taylor's music has helped me feel close to her. When the Eras Tour was announced, I desperately wanted to go to relive those memories, but I couldn't get tickets. Then, on April 27, 2023— the twelfth anniversary of my aunt's passing—a friend won tickets and gave me one. It felt like a sign from my aunt. Taylor even played a Fearless surprise song that night—the same tour my aunt once saw. I'll never forget it.

My six-year-old, Jules, wanted to go to the Eras Tour so badly. When we couldn't afford tickets, she typed up a business plan, borrowed $50, and made one thousand friendship bracelets to sell. Swifties all over the world supported her. In three days, she raised enough for floor seats in Miami and even donated to hurricane relief. We drove from Virginia to Florida to see her dream come true. It was a sparkling display of girlhood, passion, and compassion.

I've been lucky to attend a few tours, but my aunt—my second mom and the biggest Swiftie I know—had never been able to get tickets, she had only tailgated outside shows. We even threw her an Eras Tour–themed fiftieth birthday party. When she finally got tickets to the Miami show, sharing that moment with her—singing, crying, cheering—was pure magic. No matter what life brings, I'll always hold on to that memory.

Back when we were dating, I told my now-husband my dream proposal would be during "Love Story" at a Taylor Swift concert. In 2013, he made it happen! He surprised me with a trip to Minnesota and pit tickets to the Red Tour, then proposed at the exact moment in "Love Story"—and even caught it on video. We've been to every tour since, and it still brings back the best memories. I think we were one of the OG "Love Story" proposals at a Taylor concert!

One of my most personal moments as a Swiftie was hearing "I Hate It Here" for the first time. I was in a place where everything felt heavy and out of sync, like I didn't belong. Then that song came on, and it was like Taylor had put my exact feelings into words. I listened on repeat, letting the lyrics hold me. In that quiet moment, I felt seen without needing to explain a thing—and it meant more than I can say.

Being a Swiftie reunited my family. I was the first fan and introduced Taylor's music to my sisters and mom, and over time, it became something we all shared. From blasting her songs on cross-country road trips to dancing in the refrigerator light, Taylor's music helped us bond in a way we never had before.

There Wouldn't Be This If There Hadn't Been You

When you trace these precious stories—those unparalleled concert highs, the healing car rides, the friendships, the proposals, the tears of joy, the pure bliss—back to their origin, there's one constant running through them all: *Taylor Swift*. Without her, these experiences might still exist in some form. But would they be as full of magic? As beautiful? As enchanting? Her music did more than accompany our seasons of life—it transformed them. It gave them meaning. It offered us words for feelings we hadn't yet learned to name and turned ordinary days into ones we'll never forget.

If it weren't for her, I wouldn't be here writing our story. This fandom has become a defining part of who we are. It gave us a second family and a greater closeness to ourselves and each other. For that, there are millions of us who couldn't be more grateful. If these words ever reach her, let them serve as a fraction of the thank-yous she deserves to hear.

My parents bought me every CD up until 1989, even when we couldn't really afford it. There's something so comforting about growing up with Taylor—like having an older sister guiding me through life, giving me advice and teaching me the dos and don'ts of growing up.

I would thank her for speaking out about her sexual assault case—if it weren't for her, I don't think I ever would've found the courage to talk about mine. Her speech and performance of "Clean" on the Reputation Tour will always hold a special place in my heart. I'm so grateful she

chose vulnerability to help others find their strength. She gave so many of us permission to fight back.

If I could thank her for one thing, it wouldn't just be the music. I'd thank her for giving me permission to feel. For turning "too much" into a superpower. For showing me that heartbreak can be holy. That softness isn't a weakness. That I'm not alone.

I would thank her for being my one constant throughout my whole life. I've followed her since I was seven. Without her, I would be a completely different person.

I truly cannot thank her for just one thing . . . her music saved me and helped me process life's struggles—breakups, anxiety, miscarriage, grief. I wouldn't have survived without her words.

Her ability to bring people together. I use her music to connect with my students . . . and my mostly nonverbal autistic daughter loves reading her song titles in the car.

I would thank her for being there for my mom through her music—she doesn't realize it, but I think it saved her.

I would thank her for writing what I can't always say.

Thank you for helping me find my happiness and hope even when life is a daily struggle.

Being a Swiftie has made me who I am. I've listened to Taylor since day one and her music has gotten me through every single walk of life since I was sixteen. I'm now thirty-one!

I would thank Taylor for bringing my sister and I closer. I can never think of Taylor without thinking of the memories my sister and I made alongside her.

Thank you for sharing your heart, so my heart feels seen and less lonely.

Thank you for raising me—through you I stayed true to myself and never changed who I was for others.

Taylor and I are the same age, and I feel like we experienced life together at the same time. Truly thank you for having a song for every moment!

I want to thank her for creating a community that could actually save the world. A community where there is no hate and you feel safe being yourself.

I'd thank her for bringing me so much joy.

Thank you for being there when no one else was. Your music is the light in my life.

Her authenticity and bravery in putting immeasurable, remarkable, and mundane feelings into words we can all share.

So where are we today? We're still hosting Taylor-themed parties, DJ nights, and tour movie marathons. We're still gathering in the streets of New York City for album release weeks and heading to theaters for every new premiere. We're stringing friendship bracelets and deciphering easter eggs that will inevitably mark new historic days to come. We'll continue to evolve with time, and with Taylor, we'll step into new eras. But one thing will never change, and that's our admiration for her and the home she's created for all of us.

When I reach senior age, I will gladly look back at how much fun we had and the memories we made.

Her legacy will continue to live on whether she's making new music or moves on to new things.

Till death do us part, play her music at my funeral.

I will always stay for Taylor. She has always stayed for me.

Swiftie for life and my daughter will carry on the love for her!

She is timeless.

Forever and always.

When our story ends, another will begin—with new fans, new memories, and our own children carrying on what we started. The rest of the world may never fully comprehend what we were. But we will. We'll remember the times we cheered in stadiums, the nights we tuned in to livestreams, the outlandish theories that never came true, the people we found along the way, and above all, how one woman's words gave us everything we ever needed. We were there. We lived it. And we'll keep living it, through the moments we share, the songs we sing, and the traditions we pass on. What I feel for our fandom is simple, but best expressed in Taylor's own words: "And the fans, you have changed my life."

This isn't just a bridge in music history. It's an everlasting legacy. And we are, without question, *Swifties for eternity*.

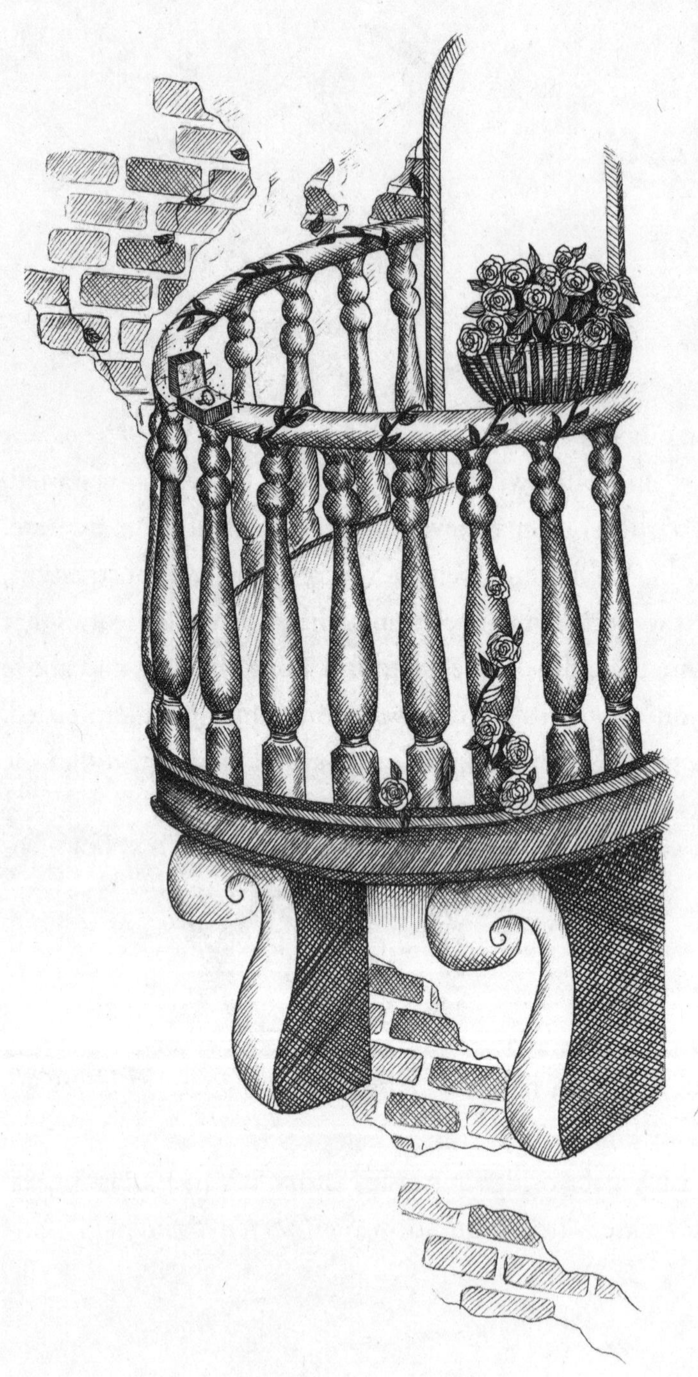

CHAPTER THIRTEEN

Long Live

Once upon a time, there was a girl, just trying to find her place in this world. On Christmas Day in 1997, she was gifted a guitar by her parents, and although she didn't quite know it yet, she was going to do so much more than just find her place in this world—she would create one of her own.

She was a dreamer. She dreamed of friendships that last a lifetime, endings that aren't too good to be true, and a love that *was really something*—not just *the idea of something*. She began writing songs that reflected these wishes, promising herself that she would never be too guarded in her music, the way she eventually had to learn to be with people. She understood her feelings at a young age and turned her pain into poetry. She had been bullied in school, and despite her best efforts to fit in, no one ever made room for her. This forced her to learn resilience at a young age. Ironically, it is also what propelled her into writing lyrics and learning chords in her bedroom all by herself, for hours on end. After putting enough pen to paper, she had written an entire catalog of songs that would eventually lead her to finding the millions of people who would make room for her. Those people were called *Swifties*, and they were *us*.

We were the hopeless romantics. The stargazers. The overthinkers and the midnight journalers. We came from everywhere, and together we built one of the most powerful communities history has ever known. We annotated the girl's albums like novels, cried over the same bridges, and studied her discography the way scholars study poetry. We waited in digital queues for hours, turned ticket drops into battlegrounds, and flew across oceans to experience the magic in person. We made friendship bracelets with lyrics, decoded secret messages in albums like we were detectives, and created our own vocabulary along the way. Through it all, we wrote a story of our own. One of loyalty, passion, depth, and above all, heart.

As she rose to fame, the girl never lost sight of what gave her the strength to keep moving forward. She knew we had been there from the start, and she never stopped showing up for us in the same way we always did for her. We felt like we knew her, because her songs told our stories. She felt like she knew us, because we made her feel understood in a way no one had before. As one, we created a space where our feelings were never questioned. At times, sure, some got carried away. But for the most part, we lived inside our own fairy tale—slaying dragons when we needed to, and building a castle that was *ours*.

Swifties meeting each other in person felt like old friends reuniting. "Catching up" wasn't necessary, because thanks to social media, we were always on the same page. We could talk for hours, even days, about the girl and the joy she brought into our lives—

our favorite songs, memories, concerts we had traveled to, blue crewnecks, cardigans, and Record Store Day vinyls we wish we had gotten before they sold out. Our language consisted of words and phrases like "koi fish guitar," "my mind is alive," and "no it's Becky." Our universe was also full of symbols like snakes, butterflies, seagulls, crowns, archers, the number thirteen, fountain pens, glitter gel pens, quill pens, autumn leaves, a red scarf, Polaroids, cowboy boots, red lipstick, and so much more. No one outside our castle could fathom any of this.

To thank us for helping her build her kingdom, the girl wanted to meet as many of us as possible, and so she did. She stood for thirteen straight hours to meet us. She invited us into her homes and introduced us to her family. She spent hours with us before and after each of her sold-out shows, and even when arenas turned into stadiums, she still kept doing it. Word got around about how talented she was, so our community just grew and grew and kept on growing. At one point, it truly felt like the entire world became a part of what we had created. At other points, it seemed like we were the only ones left. No matter what, our *castle never crumbled*. It stood strong and remained protected, because for us, being a Swiftie wasn't a fleeting moment in time or passing fad; it was eternal.

Album releases were like sacred traditions. We each listened in our own way before gathering to celebrate and discuss. Even after listening a thousand times, we would spontaneously resonate with a certain song or lyric that we hadn't paid much attention to before. We admired how she always wrote directly from her heart and soul, embracing vulnerability and honesty, without a care for whether anyone shamed her for it. It wasn't for them anyway. It was for her, and for us. Over the years, we built our own little rituals around her music—staying up until 1:58 a.m. on July 9, claiming the month of August as our own, and finding meaning in the dates and details she left tucked inside her songs.

Each album had its own aesthetic, a carefully crafted sanctuary we could step into—complete with its own mood, color palette, season, and sometimes even its own place. Some felt like autumn and winter, while others felt like spring and summer. Some made you want to pull on your favorite cardigan and curl up by the fireplace, while others made you want to *ruin the friendship* and drive to your crush's house with the windows down just to tell them you've loved them all along. They weren't just albums, they were a way of life. They helped us heal and feel alive, and became just as much a part of the eras of our lives as they were for the girl who wrote them.

We weathered every storm that came the girl's way. When the music industry tried to push her aside, she kept writing and we kept listening. When everyone else turned against her, we never did. And when the girl's past was taken from her, we walked with her into the future, helping her reclaim every piece of stolen land. One by one, re-recording by re-recording, she took back her voice, her art, and eventually the masters that should have always belonged to her. She didn't just retrace each step—she carved new ones, taking us to heights we never dreamed possible. We revisited parts of our lives we once believed were fleeting, and were given the rare gift of reliving the eras and albums that molded us—this time with greater wisdom and richer perspective. Brick by brick, we rebuilt our castle—one that stood so tall no one could ever attempt to tear it down again. It was a journey of reclamation, of rising from hardship, and of proving to the world that we were, in fact, unbreakable.

People often saw us as cultlike, even going as far as to say that the girl was a witch, and that we were just her blind followers. I can assure you that she wasn't a witch. However, she did have witchlike tendencies that even we couldn't explain—like the one time lightning struck just as she uttered the word "thunder" onstage, or when a plane soared overhead the second she sang "plane." Then there was the "Willow" performance, full of ritualistic imagery, glowing orbs, the whole thing. Really, the only true magic in those stadiums was being surrounded by eighty thousand people and still feeling like she was singing directly to you. So who knows—maybe she was a witch.

At first, it was parents bringing their children to the girl's shows—small moments that turned into lifelong memories. Over time, the audience grew. Stadiums filled with mothers and fathers, sons and daughters, partners, grandparents, and even babies wearing noise-canceling headphones. The shows swept across continents, becoming something everyone wanted—needed—to see at least once. Even if we couldn't always set foot inside the kingdom, we still found ways to feel its vibration. We gathered on hills and in parking lots, danced through rainstorms in our best dresses, and screamed every word into the night sky. We may have once imagined living in actual castles, but we were lucky enough to be living in the era of livestreams: where millions of us came together online to talk, laugh, sing, and experience the 152 shows all at once. Of those, three were canceled, and somehow, we still found a way to bring them to life. Because the magic was never only in the stage lights or the music—it lived in us too.

Just when we thought our community couldn't grow any bigger, it spilled into places we never expected. Concerts soon turned into football games, and the girl seemed to have found her Prince Charming. Having been alongside her since the beginning, we had spent decades longing for white horses, fairy tales, and epic love stories together. Now we were watching her live one of her own. What had once lived only in the girl's imagination and music video storyboards had become her reality. We showed our support by wearing red and turning Sundays into game days. Families created new traditions, while fathers and daughters discovered new ways to connect. Television commercials drew from our storylines, and Swifties filled the stands—upsetting a few dads, Brads, and Chads along the way. But this story isn't about a boy. It never was. It's about a girl—and the promise that no matter what, she'd never walk alone.

In her life, the girl faced many hardships. Yet she showed us what true perseverance and resilience mean. It was never about pretending to be okay, but about feeling every feeling and persisting anyway—even while carrying the weight of her scars. Through hard work, big dreams, and loyal support, she made us believe anything was possible. More than that, she reminded us what matters most: love, in all its forms. The kind found in romance, in friendship, in family, and in the chosen families we create, like ours.

Our story is one for the ages, unlike any other. It began with a girl who picked up a guitar, sat on her bedroom floor, and poured her heart into songs that would eventually echo across stadiums and oceans. In doing so, she united us. We turned heartbreak into healing, melodies into lifelines, and concerts into masquerade balls. We moved mountains, fought dragons, and used *all the bricks they threw at us* to forge a palace.

The girl who once felt like she didn't belong used her voice to create a space where we all did—a place where it was safe to be yourself, where it was magical to love with abandon, and where emotional honesty became a superpower. Here, music could mend hearts, connect strangers, and light up even the darkest of times. What began with one girl grew into something much greater: millions of individual stories bound together like pages of the same book. In the end, maybe that's the real fairy tale—not that we found her but that in finding each other, we found ourselves.

The girl once wrote a song called "Long Live," and we made her a promise. We vowed to keep our story alive so it would never be forgotten. So we did. We told the world of the crowds that went wild, and we made sure the names Taylor Swift and Swifties would be remembered until the end of time.

This isn't just her story. This is *The Story of Us.*

LONG
LIVE
13
FOREVER
&
ALWAYS

Swiftie Glossary: From the Vault

A curated guide to the unhinged, emotional, and wildly specific language, references, and momentous moments that define Swiftie culture.

Agency, The

Reference to the band that plays with Taylor, including longtime members such as Paul, Amos, and Mike.

Album Release Nights

The first time Taylor went to Target to buy her own album, she vlogged it—and another Swiftie tradition was born. We joined her in celebrating new releases by going to our nearest Targets at midnight for every new album release.

"Are you allergic to awesomeness?"

Something Taylor once said when an interviewer joked that the cookies she baked him made him sick.

"Are you a warrior?" / "Yes, I worry about everything."
From an interview where the reporter asked if she was a "warrior" (or "worrier," still debated). Taylor quipped, "Yes, I worry about everything." A classic fandom meme.

Athlete
Taylor Swift.

ATWTMVTVFTV
An acronym for "All Too Well (10 Minute Version) (Taylor's Version) (From the Vault)." We love talking in acronyms, but sometimes they get a little . . . extra.

Benjamin Button
Taylor's ragdoll cat, adopted after he appeared in the "ME!" music video. Always camera-ready and the most social of the three cats.

Butterfly Mural, The
April 25, 2019. The day Taylor showed up in Nashville and posed in front of a pastel butterfly mural. It was the start of the *Lover* era!

"Can you fight?"
Whenever a stunning new photo of Taylor drops, Swifties flood social media with the words "Can you fight?" usually directed at Travis Kelce. It doesn't really make sense, but the answer is always yes, he can.

Clownelia Street
Where Swifties metaphorically live after believing in a theory that didn't pan out. A play on "Cornelia Street." Population: just us.

Dead Tooth

A nickname given to Taylor by none other than Jack Antonoff after Taylor chipped her tooth on a microphone during the *Red* tour.

December 13, 1989

Taylor Swift's birthday, aka an international holiday in our calendars. Sometimes, she even gives us a gift to commemorate the day.

Dropping a Grammy

After winning too many awards at the 2010 Grammys, Taylor was photographed accidentally dropping one on the carpet.

Easter Eggs

Hidden clues in Taylor's lyrics, visuals, or public appearances. We find meaning whether it's there or not. Always has to do with her music, never her personal life.

$40 Million Legs

In 2015, it was reported that Taylor had insured her legs for $40 million. Shortly after, she posted a photo of her scratched leg—courtesy of Meredith Grey—joking that her cat now owed her $40 million.

Fountain Pen

A metaphor for Taylor's heartbreak-driven, emotionally expressive lyrics.

Fourth of July

Taylor is known for hosting Fourth of July parties at her Rhode Island home. In 2016, photos of her and her friends running into the ocean went viral. In 2023, she posted about being "independent girlies" and wrote, "see you tonight Kansas Cityyy." In hindsight, that moment was the spark before everything changed, since Travis Kelce attended the Kansas City Eras Tour show that weekend.

George Washington

A bird that frequently visited Taylor's Rhode Island house. She casually named him George Washington—and we took it very seriously.

Glitter Gel Pen

Represents Taylor's fun, poppy, sparkly lyrics.

Gold Noodle Dress

We came up with many nicknames for Taylor's outfits during the Eras Tour. This one in particular was associated with one of the *Fearless* era dresses she wore.

Got a Lot of Starbucks Lovers

The most famous Taylor lyric mishear. Fans, and even Scott Swift, heard "Blank Space" the first time and thought she sang "got a lot of Starbucks lovers" instead of "got a long list of ex-lovers."

"Help, I'm still at the restaurant"

A line used by fans when they miss something dearly—like the Eras Tour. This one has even made its way outside the fandom!

"Hey guys it's Dibbles"

Taylor named one of her cats Olivia but said that her real personality screams "Dibbles."

"Hey kids, spelling is fun!"
Part of the original bridge of "ME!" It was eventually cut from the song but we managed to keep it alive. Gone but never forgotten.

How She Holds a Pen
Taylor holds her pen between her index and middle fingers and fans always make fun of her for it.

"I say, 'That's my baby, and I'm real proud'"
A phrase Andrea Swift once said about Taylor. We now use it whenever Taylor breaks yet another record—or when she does just about anything, really.

"I think for me, um . . ."
Taylor's go-to phrase in interviews for years. She even once acknowledged she said it too often—before accidentally starting to say it again and laughing at herself, and we all thought it was hilarious.

Itty Bitty Pretty Kitty Committee, The
The name Taylor came up with for her furry children.

"I would very much like to be excluded from this narrative"
An iconic line from Taylor's 2016 Notes app statement. We now say it whenever we want to bow out of drama or distance ourselves from something.

"Je suis calme!"

Taylor speaking French in the "ME!" music video. Swifties quote it when telling themselves to calm down—usually while doing the opposite.

Karen

The inflatable snake from the *Reputation* Stadium Tour. She slithered, she served, and yes—Taylor named her.

Kitty Finlay

Andrea Swift's Great Dane . . . and the inspiration for the character named in "The Life of a Showgirl" track.

Lyrics That Could Cut Glass

After a *reputation* Secret Session, one fan on Tumblr said the lyrics to "Gorgeous" could "cut glass." It's a fantastic song, but out of all the genius writing on the album, fans thought it was funny that *that's* the one that stood out the most. We never let it go.

Meredith Grey

Taylor's original Scottish fold cat, named after the *Grey's Anatomy* character. Often looks perpetually done with everything.

Nils Sjöberg

The pseudonym she's used, which she said she picked because it's a combination of two common names in Sweden.

"Not a lot going on at the moment"

The phrase originally printed on the white T-shirt Taylor wears in the "22" music video. Years later, she used it again as the caption of an Instagram post in April 2020, while secretly working on *folklore* and *evermore*. At the time, we took it at face value, not realizing it was one of her most masterful easter eggs.

Olivia Benson

Another Scottish fold, named after a character in *Law & Order: SVU*. Loves to pose like a meerkat. Very well-behaved.

"Omg did you just call me 'daddy'"

The most insane thing Taylor has ever tweeted.

Quill Pen

Taylor's term for her most poetic, literary songwriting.

Red Herring

Sometimes used to mislead Swifties. In February 2024, a jumbled word—"hneriergrd"—appeared on Taylor's website. We quickly unscrambled it to read "red herring," and many of us thought it hinted at a *reputation (Taylor's Version)* announcement. However, it was a distraction: The true clue was a different code, "DPT: 321," which led us to *The Tortured Poets Department* album announcement that night at the Grammys. Since then, we always question if Taylor's playing mind games . . .

Royal Family Hard Launch

The first time Travis made it onto Taylor's Instagram page was a selfie with the royal family on June 22, 2024.

***SNL* Monologue**

When Taylor hosted *Saturday Night Live* in 2009, she opened the show with a self-written musical monologue. It was peak comedy and one of her most highlighted TV appearances.

"Sooo excited. This is the main event."

A behind-the-scenes clip from the "Karma" music video. We use it anytime Taylor does literally anything headline-worthy.

"So over the years . . ."

From the *1989* deluxe album, where "New Romantics" ends and Taylor suddenly starts explaining her writing process in the first voice memo. It usually catches us off guard.

Starlights, The

Taylor's four gorgeous backup singers: Jeslyn, Eliotte, Kamilah, and Melanie.

"Stars do u like dem"

A Tumblr moment when a fan said "taylor what is this" to her abstract drawings of stars. She responded with "Stars do u like dem."

Stella McCartney Pop-Up

Taylor surprised fans by showing up at the New York City pop-up shop for her *Lover* collaboration with Stella McCartney in 2019. She did the same for her *reputation* NYC pop-up in 2017.

"Swift af boi"

During the Cincinnati, Ohio, Eras Tour show in June 2023, a mechanical lift failed during a costume-change moment. Taylor quickly ran across the stage to continue the show. Later, she commented "still swift af boi" in response to a video of it.

Taydaughter

An artist mentored or championed by Taylor.

Tayimpact

The cultural ripple Taylor creates. From football viewership to friendship bracelets, she moves the needle.

Taylor Hates *evermore*

A fandom joke based on how rarely she acknowledges the album. She's addressed it on the Eras Tour, but it still lives on.

Taylor Tots

What we call the little, young, adorable Swifties.

Taylurking

When Taylor secretly (or not-so-secretly) views, likes, or stalks Swifties online.

Tayprincess
Used whenever Taylor looks like a princess.

Tayroomba
Nickname for the Roomba-style device that glided Taylor across the stage in "Who's Afraid of Little Old Me?" during the Eras Tour.

Tayvis / TNT
Nicknames for Taylor and Travis. Tayvis = fandom started. TNT = Taylor and Travis started.

Tayvoodoo
The mysterious force that makes things fall perfectly into place for Taylor.

"Thank you for saying that"
Taylor's sweet, automatic response to compliments. I think some of us have even added it to our own vocabulary without realizing it . . . I know I did!

Thirteen
Taylor's lucky number and now a sacred symbol in our community. She intentionally makes everything add up to thirteen. You'll find it everywhere, including on our hands at concerts: something Taylor did when she first began touring.

"Thug Story"
Taylor's hilarious parody rap with T-Pain at the CMT Awards in 2009. Forever legendary.

Track Five
The most emotionally devastating song on every album. We always know it's coming, yet we're still never prepared.

Triskaidekaphilia
The official term for Taylor's obsession with the number thirteen.

Very First Swiftie, The
A fan named Holly is often remembered as the "first Swiftie." She was photographed with Taylor on the boardwalk in Point Pleasant, New Jersey, when they were both about thirteen years old. Nearly two decades later, Taylor invited Holly to the *Lover* Secret Session to reunite and thank her for being there from the very beginning.

Waglor
A fandom nickname from Taylor's football era, combining "WAG" (wives and girlfriends of athletes) with Taylor's name. It playfully refers to Taylor embracing her role as an NFL WAG with Travis Kelce.

Theories: From the Vault

Suitcase Day

That day in 2017 when everyone thought Taylor was being carried out of her NYC apartment in a suitcase to avoid paparazzi. The mystery has never truly been solved.

The Lost *Karma* Album

Swifties were convinced there was a scrapped album called *Karma* (color-coded orange) that Taylor replaced with *reputation*. The word "karma" appeared on the wall in "The Man" music video, fueling the legend.

Five Holes in the Fence

A failed theory from early 2019, sparked by a daily sequence of posts Taylor shared as she shifted from her darker *Rep* era into a brighter *Lover* aesthetic. Fans noticed Meredith on a couch with eight indents, an image of seven palm trees, Taylor sitting on the sixth step of a staircase, and her face behind a fence with five holes—and thought it was a countdown to an announcement. When nothing appeared on the "day four" post, everyone joked she had "four-gotten." No announcement was made, and the countdown was entirely unintentional, giving rise to the phrase "But there were five holes in the fence!" Later that year, five days before *Lover*'s release, Taylor reposted the fence photo with "Okay NOW there are five holes in the fence," cementing the joke in Swiftie lore.

Lover House

First appearing in the "Lover" music video, the *Lover* House is believed to represent Taylor's first ten albums, with each room symbolizing a different era. The tenth, *Midnights*, is reflected in the starry night sky surrounding the house. The *Lover* House later reappeared on the Eras Tour, where it dramatically burns down during the *1989* era.

Woodvale

One *folklore* deluxe cover had the mysterious word "woodvale" written across it. Fans thought it meant a third secret album was coming—until Taylor explained it was just a code name left on the mock-up by mistake.

evermore Long Pond Sessions

We got a *folklore: The Long Pond Studio Sessions* film, but never one for *evermore*. Some fans still think it exists, but it may stay in the vault forever.

The *Red* Scarf

For years, fans believed there really was a scarf left behind, and theories swirled about whether it was ever returned. It became one of the most enduring symbols in Swiftie lore. During a Q & A at TIFF in 2022, Taylor revealed it was always meant as a metaphor. But . . . we'll still always wonder, won't we?

Cake Numbers in "I Bet You Think About Me"

The cake layers in the music video were dissected for meaning. Theories settled on 26, since it was track 26 on *Red (Taylor's Version)*, and of course, 13, no explanation needed.

Midnights Mayhem (Upside-Down Phone)

When revealing *Midnights* track titles, Taylor pulled names from a bingo cage and held up a corded phone—sometimes upside down. Swifties dissected the meaning, but ultimately . . . it meant nothing.

"Karma" Music Video Coffee Cup

In BTS footage from the "Karma" video, Taylor held a coffee cup while wearing blue nail polish on one thumb and black nail polish on the other. Fans swore it was signaling an upcoming announcement of *1989 (Taylor's Version)* and *reputation (Taylor's Version)*.

Haunted Piano

During the Eras Tour, Taylor's piano started playing by itself, and her genuine shock onstage had fans convinced it was haunted.

No LA Post

Taylor made thank-you posts on social media for every Eras Tour city except Los Angeles. Fans speculated she was planning a secret extension of the tour there, but it seems she may have simply forgotten . . . or maybe it was a red herring.

The Monkey

Fans spotted what looked like a monkey and a white dress stored under the Eras Tour stage. To this day, no one knows why it was there.

Taylor Nation Going Live

One random night during the Eras Tour, Taylor Nation went live on Instagram, making us think something big was happening. Fans speculated that it might have been an intern's mistake . . .

Taylor on the Bleachers

During an Eras Tour opener, a blurry fan photo seemed to show Taylor sitting in the bleachers. Was it really her watching the show like one of us? We may never know . . . but the mystery will haunt us forever.

Double *1989* Outfit Color Combos

On the Eras Tour, Taylor rotated her *1989* two-piece sets in different colors but skipped the green/green and green/yellow versions. Fans theorized she was saving them for a big announcement like *reputation (Taylor's Version)* or *Taylor Swift (Taylor's Version)*.

Santa Claus Backstage

At the final Eras Tour show in Vancouver, Santa and an elf were spotted backstage. Fans thought they'd join Taylor onstage, but they never did. Likely just crew members being festive.

The Orange Door

On the final night of the Eras Tour, Taylor chose to exit through an orange door. We didn't all know it at the time, but we were less than a year away from entering our new era.

Pinocchio Theory

When Taylor said *The Life of a Showgirl* would have only twelve tracks, fans thought she was lying because there was a Pinocchio in the background.

Sourdough Super Bowl Theory

Taylor went on and on about sourdough bread in the *New Heights* podcast interview, and Swifties thought it hinted she'd perform the following halftime show at Levi's Stadium, home of the 49ers—whose mascot is Sourdough Sam.

"The Black Dog" Meaning

Taylor teased that no one fully understands the true meaning of "The Black Dog." She insisted it's not just about a bar, sparking endless speculation.

Exit Signs

Double exit signs appeared in many of the clips and images from *The Life of a Showgirl* promo before its release. At first, some thought they were nothing more than background details—but *none of it was accidental*. The double exits became the symbol of a double goodbye: marking the official close of the Eras Tour era and ushering in *The Final Show*, along with a six-part series chronicling Taylor's life behind the curtain of the most historic tour of all time.

Dear Swifties,

While the glossary, dates, and theories on the previous pages capture some of our most memorable moments, there are far too many to ever fit in this book—and countless more still to come. Each inside joke, every wild prediction, and all the phrases we've carried with us along the way tell the story of who we are.

Make sure you write them all down here, so they'll always remain a part of our history.

Forever & Always,
Olivia

Acknowledgments

Writing this book was the unexpected journey of a lifetime—one made possible by so many people who believed in me, inspired me, and helped bring this story into the world.

To Taylor, thank you for being the spark that lit the match, igniting a passion and a community that I'll carry with me for the rest of my life. But mostly, thank you for being you. Because of everything you've created and because of your heart, I found my path, my people, and the story I was meant to tell.

To the Swifties—those I've chatted with online and in person, those who've followed me for years, and those who've recently joined our fandom—thank you for trusting me with your memories, your experiences, and, above all, *our story.* You are the reason our community feels like home, and this book only exists because of you.

To my parents, thank you for having faith in me long before I ever learned to have it in myself. Maman, thank you for becoming a Swiftie with me. From every show we attended together to the memory of sitting on Taylor's living room floor listening to *reputation* for the first time—an experience I wouldn't have wanted to share with anyone else—these are moments I will treasure forever. Your guidance and natural creative eye were invaluable in designing the cover and illustrations; this book wouldn't be what it is without your input on every little decision. Dad, thank you for your unwavering support, for sitting with me and watching endless YouTube videos, for listening to my heartfelt reflections on Taylor's music, and for trusting me to follow a path that wasn't always traditional. To you both, thank you for taking me to concerts in different cities, for letting me travel on my own and chase the experiences that shaped this story, and for continuously encouraging me to take risks and dream bigger. Most importantly, you gave me the freedom to explore my passions and, ultimately, myself. Your love and encouragement have carried me through every step of this unpredictable journey.

To my brother Gabriel, thank you for finally giving in to the Swiftie way of life and for always keeping tabs on Taylor's latest broken records (I think you beat the headlines every time). To my brother Jeremy, thank you for letting me slip Taylor songs between your rock playlists and for always listening, even to a world you know little about. And a special thank-you to Patrick, who has become like a third brother to me and has also been a steady, reassuring light in my life.

To Aunt Phyllis and Uncle Jonathan—thank you for always being there for me, for following along, even downloading Instagram just to like my posts, and for supporting me in your own loving ways.

À mes grands-parents, Majo et Daniel, en France—merci pour votre ouverture d'esprit, votre curiosité et la façon dont vous avez toujours accueilli tout ce que je fais, même à des kilomètres de distance. Malgré la barrière de la langue, vous avez suivi mon parcours avec tant de fierté, partagé mes dernières nouvelles avec tous ceux qui vous entourent, téléchargé Instagram juste pour liker mes posts et regardé tous les films des concerts avec moi. J'ai tellement hâte de vous traduire ce livre. Je vous aime tellement.

To Sophia, my roommate and one of my greatest friends—thank you for being the first to read this book, for listening to every idea and every spiral, and for cheering me on along the way. Even if you'll never officially call yourself a Swiftie, you've embraced my passion fully, and that means so much. To Casey, thank you for letting me pull you into the fandom in college and for staying up with me on the streets of New York City that one unforgettable night. To Jacenda, my childhood best friend, who witnessed the early days of my fangirl phase during countless sleepovers—*thank you for bearing with me.* And to all my family and friends who follow along simply because they care, even if Taylor isn't their genre: Your support has never gone unnoticed.

To my agents, Larry and Sascha, thank you for believing in my vision for this story and for caring about it just as much as I do. To my editor, Maria, this book would not be what it is without you and your ability to understand exactly what I wanted it to become. It has been such a joy revisiting so many special memories with you along the way. And to Cian, whose illustrations captured the magic of these pages—thank you for portraying the spirit of our universe so beautifully. I feel incredibly lucky that every one of you is a Swiftie, because it means this book was created by people who truly understand its heartbeat, and I couldn't have done it with anyone else. Lastly, thank you to the marketing and publicity team, production team, art department, and every single person at Simon & Schuster who had a hand in bringing our fandom's story to life!